Public Spending
and Postwar
Economic Policy

Public Spending

and Postwar Economic Policy

By SHERWOOD M. FINE

COLUMBIA UNIVERSITY PRESS · NEW YORK
1944

COPYRIGHT 1944 COLUMBIA UNIVERSITY PRESS, NEW YORK
Foreign Agent: OXFORD UNIVERSITY PRESS, Humphrey Milford, Amen House, London, E.C., 4, England, AND B. I. Building, Nicol Road, Bombay, India
MANUFACTURED IN THE UNITED STATES OF AMERICA

PREFACE

THE PRESENT STUDY had its genesis in the author's interest, while he was a member of the staff of the Division of Monetary Research of the United States Treasury Department, in the development of federal spending measures seeking to combat the course of the 1937 recession. The great controversy at that time between the advocates of expansionist public spending and the "budget balancers" vividly revealed the absence of agreement which reigned in the field of fiscal policy. The admixture of theoretical improvisation and political expediency apparent in the conflicting arguments underscored the tentative character of our knowledge in this area. An opportunity to undertake a more general study in the field of public spending was offered in the form of a Littauer Fellowship at Harvard University during the academic year 1939–1940.

In the Fiscal Policy Seminar of the Harvard Graduate School of Public Administration, presided by Professor Alvin H. Hansen and Professor John H. Williams, an opportunity was afforded to examine various issues of this youthful discipline. The original plan of the volume was enlarged from an appraisal of New Deal emergency spending policy to an examination of the scope and place of compensatory public spending in our economy. The intervention of World War II prompted a further reorientation of the study in the direction of postwar economic policy.

The author wishes to acknowledge the kind assistance first of Professor J. M. Clark who made many helpful suggestions at various stages of the writing of the volume. Thanks are gratefully extended to Professor Carl S. Shoup and Professor Robert Murray Haig, of Columbia University, who read the original manuscript and offered many helpful criticisms. The writer's indebtedness to Professor Hansen is especially great and is in no wise adequately indicated in the text. I am also indebted to Robert R. Nathan, of the War Production Board, Harvey S. Perloff, of the Federal Reserve Board, Arthur E. Burns, of the National Bureau of Economic Research, Benjamin Ginzburg and Ben Caplan, of the Office of Price Administration, Reid Denis and Lloyd Metzler, of Harvard University, who read all or parts of the manuscript and submitted useful criticisms. Full responsibility for the present study is, of course, assumed by the author. The manuscript was edited by Miss Ida M. Lynn, of the Columbia University Press.

January 5, 1944
Washington, D. C.

CONTENTS

I. **INTRODUCTION** ... 1
　The Stagnation Thesis ... 1
　The Rise of Fiscal Policy ... 2
　New Deal Economic Policy and Results ... 3
　War Expenditures and Full Employment ... 4
　Scope of Volume ... 5

II. **THE EMERGENCE OF FISCAL POLICY** ... 6
　Public Works Planning ... 8
　Pump-Priming ... 12
　The Multiplier ... 14
　Pump-Priming (continued) ... 22

III. **COMPENSATORY PUBLIC SPENDING AND SECULAR-STAGNATION** ... 29
　Mr. Keynes and Unemployment ... 31
　Mr. Hansen and Secular-Stagnation ... 34
　Compensatory Public Spending ... 36
　The Capital-Current Budget ... 40

IV. **A CRITIQUE OF SECULAR-STAGNATION DOCTRINE** ... 45
　Economic Progress and Technological Saturation ... 45
　Population Growth and New Investment ... 56
　Investment Opportunities and the Limits of Economic Penetration ... 63

V. **THE LIMITS TO PUBLIC DEBT** ... 67
　The Relativity of Public Debt ... 73
　Public Debt and the Threat to Private Enterprise ... 80

VI. **PUBLIC SPENDING, 1933–1940** ... 86
　From the Inauguration to WPA ... 88
　The Meaning of WPA ... 95
　Deficits and Budgets ... 99
　Subsidized Recovery ... 101
　The 1937 Recession ... 107

CONTENTS

Policy, Spending and Results	115
Recovery Policy Takes a Back Seat	122

VII. THE LESSONS OF NEW DEAL SPENDING — 124
Results — 124
Tax Policy and Spending Policy — 126
The Volume of Public Spending — 127
Is Spending the Cure? — 128
The Ideology of Spending — 130
Emergency Public Works — 133
Public and Private Construction — 136
Self-Liquidating Public Projects — 138
Summary — 140

VIII. PUBLIC SPENDING AND POSTWAR ECONOMIC POLICY — 141
Introduction — 141
The Short-Run Problem — 141
The Prospects — 144
Public Policy in the Transition Period — 147
The Post-Transitional Period — 151
The Role of Public Spending — 154
International Economic Policy — 157

BIBLIOGRAPHY — 161

INDEX — 171

TABLES AND CHARTS

TABLES

1.	Percentage of Tax Collections to National Income	52
2.	Estimated Expenditure of Public Funds for New Public Construction, 1930–1940	98
3.	Federal Expenditures and Receipts, Calendar Years 1936–1937	112
4.	National Defense Expenditures	122
5.	Distribution of Gross National Product	142

CHARTS

I.	Successive Stages of Income Produced by a Single Investment Outlay	17
II.	Successive Stages of Income Produced by Continued Investment Outlays	18
III.	Successive Stages of Income Produced by Six Investment Outlays	19
IV.	Net Contribution of the Federal Government to National Buying Power	92
V.	The Federal Net Contribution and Economic Activity	93
VI.	Expenditures for Construction of Federal Public Works Classified according to Function, Fiscal Years 1921–1941	135
VII.	Estimated Volume of New Construction Activity in the United States, and Federal Expenditures and Guaranties for New Construction, 1920–1940	137

I. INTRODUCTION

THE DEEP CONCERN manifested by the democratic peoples of the world over the shape of postwar reconstruction, particularly with respect to programs for economic rehabilitation, in the midst of a war which is far from won, is testimony to the insecurity which has plagued us in the past. For despite the many virtues of democratic liberalism, capitalism has provided neither economic stability nor the assurance of freedom from want so prominent in the aspirations of the common man. Out of the great conflict is arising the fervent conviction that the democracies cannot return to their prewar status. The world is searching for a positive implementation of the promise of democracy. The choice between freedom on the one hand and security on the other presented during the nineteen thirties is increasingly suspect. The common man is asking: "Must freedom be purchased by exposure to poverty and insecurity? Cannot society shape its own course?" The challenge of the future is clear. Very little agreement, however, characterizes the various recommendations for securing the desired objectives. The present volume is addressed to the consideration of some of the major problems of domestic economic rehabilitation. A critical appraisal of the economic policies and theories of the last decade affords an indispensable orientation for postwar policy.

THE STAGNATION THESIS

Largely as a result of the depression of the nineteen thirties serious doubt has arisen over the ability of our economic institutions to achieve reasonably full utilization of resources in the postwar period. Between World War I and World War II there has taken place a profound psychological reorientation toward the future of capitalist enterprise. The period before and after World War I enjoyed expanding investment opportunities and rising income levels and, above all, was characterized by an unswerving optimism over the future. The decade prior to World War II, in contrast, suffered great idle capacity and unemployment. Professor Alvin Hansen's secular-stagnation doctrine [1] gave eloquent expression to the pessimism which

[1] See *Full Recovery or Stagnation?* and *Fiscal Policy and Business Cycles*.

enveloped that period. The dismal decade of the thirties was described by Professor Hansen as an expression of a long-run alteration in the character of our economy. In essence, it is held that we are suffering the consequences of economic maturity. This development is marked by reduced opportunity for private investment in capital-absorbing industries, the disappearance of undeveloped areas, and a decline in the rate of population growth.

Professor Hansen proposes that the secular decline in private investment opportunities be met by public investment, primarily in noncompetitive fields. Government outlay is the necessary expedient to combat idle resources. The public sector of the economy must be expanded, with no predictable limit. We must accept a shift in the relative importance of government to private enterprise. The costs involved are to be financed in good part by additions to the national debt.

The implications of the above position for the whole system of private enterprise are profound. It is hence entirely understandable that the secular-stagnation thesis and the proposed fiscal curative (which is, however, by no means chained to the stagnation viewpoint) have been the subject of vigorous controversy. The unfortunate tendency for participants in the dispute over fiscal policy to take extreme positions has tended to obscure the scope and the place of this instrument of control. Doctrinaire views on both sides have served to obfuscate the basic issues.

THE RISE OF FISCAL POLICY

The character of disagreement over fiscal policy reflects in good part the relatively immature development of this body of theory as well as the inconclusive outcome of the spending program of the Roosevelt administration. The field of fiscal policy, which in some respects represents a continuation, on a broader scale, of central banking policy,[2] was only slightly explored prior to the decade of the thirties. Public finance treatises devoted but scant attention to the economic consequences of public expenditures or to the effects of the tax system upon business activity. Theories of public spending in the older public finance treatises were imperfectly developed and not related conceptually to the operation of the economic system as a whole.

[2] See John H. Williams, "Federal Budget: Economic Consequences of Deficit Financing," *American Economic Review*, XXX, No. 5 (Supplement, February, 1941), p. 55.

INTRODUCTION 3

The advent of the depression precipitated a great deal of interest in the field of fiscal policy. The rapid expansion of public outlays, necessitated by large-scale unemployment, forcibly raised the issue of the extent to which these expenditures constituted a dynamic element in the economic environment. The practical end of fiscal policy became increasingly concerned with the analysis of the relation between public fiscal operations and business activity, while the theory of fiscal policy sought to establish the position of fiscal operations as a part of the general theory of the functioning of our economy.

J. M. Keynes, in his *General Theory of Employment, Interest and Money*, offered an analytical system in which public fiscal operations are assigned an integral place. Keynes's "propensity to consume" is treated as the most important of the three psychological propensities which combine to determine the level of employment and income. The government, by influencing the volume of consumption, directly affects the aggregate level of national income. The multiplier establishes the relationship between primary increments of investment and secondary or induced consumption.

NEW DEAL ECONOMIC POLICY AND RESULTS

The severity of the depression inherited by the Roosevelt administration prompted the adoption of various unorthodox policies. The discrediting of central banking policy during the latter part of the Hoover administration left the succeeding administration without any generally accepted means for combating the depression. Expansionist public spending emerged from the caldron of New Deal economic measures as the chief instrument of recovery policy.[3] The picture of Roosevelt fiscal policy is complicated by constant reformulations in the program pursued along with revisions in the theoretical rationale. This performance aptly reflected the substantial disagreement and uncertainty within the administration as well as pressure to

[3] John H. Williams would deny the term "policy" to the successive spending measures of the Roosevelt administration: "There is no evidence that the administration, as distinct from some persons within it and some economists offering advice from the outside, ever had a conscious interest in fiscal policy as an instrument of recovery prior to the new depression in 1938. Government spending was primarily for relief and was regarded mainly as the unavoidable accompaniment of unemployment until recovery could be achieved by other means."—"The Implications of Fiscal Policy for Monetary Policy and the Banking System," *American Economic Review*, XXXII (Supplement, March, 1942), 234-249. The writer, while agreeing as to the pre-eminence of relief spending, believes that various decisions made prior to 1938 can be attributed to a conscious fiscal policy. See Chapter VI.

rationalize, for public consumption, the wisdom of the measures pursued. The formal justification of public spending has deviated so greatly from the character of the programs actually followed that it has confused inevitably the nature of the successive fiscal programs.

The stated objective of New Deal relief and recovery outlays was never realized. Despite the great expenditures, our economy continued to suffer from substantial idle resources. Unemployment figures averaged over ten million per annum throughout the period 1933–1940.[4] Not until 1937 did any appreciable volume of new private capital investment comparable to that of the late twenties materialize. The failure of business enterprise to revive has been blamed in large part upon ill-advised federal fiscal policies.[5] On the other hand, the incomplete recovery realized during the thirties has been attributed by advocates of aggressive public spending to defective fiscal planning and inadequate measures. Spending, it is alleged, has been far short of the magnitude required for recovery; the administration, moreover, has adopted tax measures inconsistent with the spending objectives; finally, the entire program has been poorly timed.[6]

WAR EXPENDITURES AND FULL EMPLOYMENT

Unfortunately, the great dispute over New Deal public spending was never resolved. The outbreak of war temporarily eclipsed the debate. The relief and recovery programs of the Roosevelt administration were succeeded first by a defense program and an aid-to-Britain program and subsequently by enormously expanded war appropriations. These latter outlays, which dwarfed by far the relatively modest depression expenditures, have transformed our economy from one with substantial unutilized resources to one suffering shortages of most resources. What moderate peacetime public spending failed to achieve, greatly enlarged wartime spending has accomplished.

War outlays are, in a sense, carrying to logical fruition the expansionist spending doctrines expressed during the thirties. But, to force the obvious, no such military expenditure program can be submitted as a peacetime solution to the problem of low national income, although some contend that the direction may be indicated by the

[4] See chart "Estimates of Unemployment," appearing monthly in the *Social Security Bulletin* of the Social Security Board.
[5] Cf. Sumner H. Slichter, "The Period 1919–1936 in the United States: Its Significance for Business Cycle Theory," *Review of Economic Statistics*, XIX (February, 1937), 1–19.
[6] Cf. Burns and Watson. *Government Spending and Economic Expansion.*

INTRODUCTION

results of war spending. In the postwar period our economy, freed from enormous war outlays, may bog down; once again we may be confronted with the necessity of formulating a national economic program capable of securing relatively full utilization of resources. What role may be assigned to fiscal policy?

SCOPE OF VOLUME

The present study is primarily concerned with establishing the proper scope and place of fiscal policy in postwar economic policy. This analysis necessarily involves an appraisal of the factors contributing to underutilization of resources. How valid is the Hansenian secular-stagnation theory? Is it more apparent than real? A critical appraisal of the stagnation doctrine will assist in the clarification of the scope of fiscal policy. An analysis of the spending measures of the Roosevelt administration provides a useful frame of reference into the short-run effects and problems involved in such a program. The problem of debt is investigated to determine to what extent limits in this area control freedom of action in the realm of fiscal operations. We are told that "a public debt of $4,000 billion *may* be carried by the economy without a collapse of the capitalist system, a repudiation of the debt, or a great inflation." [7] Perhaps our children or grandchildren will live to see a national debt of that size. If they do, it will not necessarily prove or disprove the wisdom of those who advocated unrestricted deficit financing.

The following study is viewed primarily as a contribution to a clarification and synthesis of the various institutional and structural problems impinging upon public spending policy and the extent to which such policy may be used to achieve fuller utilization of resources. Chapter II provides the setting for the discussion of more recent theory.

[7] Harris, ed., *Postwar Economic Problems*, p. 184.

II. THE EMERGENCE OF FISCAL POLICY

THE MARSHALING of economic arguments to support enlarged government outlays is a comparatively modern development. While certain categories of public expenditure, such as direct relief and work relief programs, have typically risen in periods of crises or depression, they have rarely, until recently, been thought of as *positive* aspects of government economic policy. Discussions of public expenditures in the classical literature have never given adequate thought to the relationship of changing levels of outlay to the general economic situation. The sterility of theoretical studies in this field is explained in part by the statement that "the older English writers did not need a theory of expenditures because the theory of government which they held implied a fixed limit to governmental functions." [1] Adam Smith's dictum that the range of public activities properly the province of the sovereign, was restricted to (1) defense, (2) the establishment of justice, and (3) erection and maintenance of certain public works [2] remained long unchallenged in theory, although the scope of government widened greatly during the nineteenth century. Not until the business cycle had come to be recognized as a characteristic phenomenon [3] was it pertinent to find an *economic* justification for enlarged emergency expenditures.

Both the size and the character of governmental expenditures underwent revolutionary changes during the nineteenth and twentieth centuries. The details of the story of the impact of social, political, and economic change on the expenditure pattern of governments (and vice versa) provide some of the most interesting chapters in the history of the growth and development of capitalist economies.[4] Unfortunately, we cannot trace here the effects on public spending of such changes as (1) the rise of large industrial cities, involving the introduction of a host of new and very expensive government func-

[1] Adams, *Science of Finance*, p. 53.
[2] *Wealth of Nations* (Everyman's ed.), II, 180–181.
[3] Mitchell, *Business Cycles*, chap. ii.
[4] The literature in this field is too voluminous to warrant detailed references. For selective references see Bullock, *Selected Readings in Public Finance*, 2d ed., chaps. ii and iii.

THE EMERGENCE OF FISCAL POLICY

tions, such as sanitation, education, protection of water supply, recreation, and so forth; (2) the growth of democracy which was responsible for making governments increasingly sensitive to the demands of the population for an ever-widening variety of services. This development has found expression, in part, in the organization of "pressure groups," such as veterans' and farmers' organizations, chambers of commerce, and the like, serving as effective instruments for maximizing their share of the total public outlay; (3) the growth of economic insecurity, which has had to be met by large appropriations for unemployment relief and insurance, old age pensions, and so forth; (4) the rise of modern war expenditures,[5] aided by the recent development of widespread soldiers' pensions, bonuses, and so forth. Another very important explanation for the aggregate rise in public outlay has been the unprecedented expansion in population during the last century and a half.

Expenditures for public works [6] have come to represent a larger and larger aggregate item in total public outlays. The growing demand for public improvements has found expression in both extensive and intensive expansion of government services.

The aggregate volume of public works has naturally increased through the ages with the material and technical advance of mankind, although discontinuously with the rise and fall of great civilizations, being clearly greater during eras of high material achievement than in earlier periods of growth and later ages of relapse or decay. Until perhaps the eighteenth century, the amount of public construction in the western world could barely have been of comparable magnitude with that of the Roman world in its prime. With the spread of the Industrial Revolution, private and public construction alike must have rapidly expanded. Yet, in the earlier stages of this process of economic transformation the relative volume of public works may well have declined as the economic functions of government were narrowly circumscribed under the influence of the dominant philosophy of "laissez-faire." With the decline of this economic philosophy, however, and with the state's progressive assumption of additional economic functions, this tendency has been reversed and the volume of public works has grown both absolutely and relatively to private construction.[7]

---

[5] The progressive mechanization of military operations has resulted in making each successive war more expensive than its predecessor. The per capita outlay for the American Army of World War II, for example, is considerably greater than for World War I.

[6] "Public works" may be defined as all durable goods, primarily fixed structures, produced by government. The provision of intangible services is ordinarily excluded from this category. Cf. Clark, *The Economics of Planning Public Works*, p. 2.

[7] A. Gayer, *Public Works in Prosperity and Depression*, pp. 20–21.

PUBLIC WORKS PLANNING

The pace at which the absolute growth of public works proceeded was in the long run determined by the broad considerations mentioned above. The short-run variations in expenditures by governments were determined more by fiscal ability than by the relative urgency of various types of projects. On the whole, short-run variations in public-works activity have followed fluctuations in the level of economic activity. As a rule more public works have been constructed in times of prosperity than in times of depression.[8] Public works expenditures have usually risen in prosperous periods, stimulated by the prevalent optimism and supported by increasing revenue as well as willingness and ability to resort to borrowing. State and local governments suffer in depression periods from impaired revenues as well as from increased difficulty in obtaining credit. This situation could only be modified by the introduction of a system of planned public works or, more properly, public works planned differently from the manner they have been in the past. The relative absence of freedom on the part of local governments in decisions concerning the timing of public works also reflected the existence of a backlog of necessary public facilities, in part attributable to the absence of planning. It is difficult to advocate curtailment of public works activities in prosperous periods, when important deficiencies exist in the provision of various services.[9]

In general, stabilization plans did not provide for any increase in total public works expenditures over the duration of a complete cycle. Rather, a *given* volume of outlay was to be *strategically* timed.

The origin of the various plans for utilizing public works as a stabilizing factor through strategic timing of outlays is rather obscure. While the theoretical props of the proposal were not formulated with any clarity until comparatively recently, we know that in the past governments were obliged to yield to public pressure for expanded emergency construction in depression and crisis periods as the most simple method of creating work for the unemployed.[10] Despite the apparent practical economic advantages of such activities, public

[8] *Ibid.*, p. 3.

[9] Bielschowsky, "*Business Fluctuations and Public Works,*" *Quarterly Journal of Economics*, XLIV (February, 1930), 311.

[10] Public works relief projects date back to the early Egyptian era. Because of the annual overflowing of the Nile, there was a three-month period in which peasants were unable to cultivate the fields. Modern historians have come to believe that enforced labor

THE EMERGENCE OF FISCAL POLICY

bodies have failed to profit from these opportunities to build up their capital equipment. The absence of public works planning and the characteristic wasteful administration reflected the popular belief that these employment-creating schemes were nothing more than make-work programs.[11] These programs, usually undisguised poor-relief schemes, resulted frequently in a minimum of necessary public works. Another basic difficulty with improvised public works was that they were seldom sufficiently large to absorb any appreciable number of unemployed.[12]

A. L. Bowley, the statistician, in a Poor Law report in 1909,[13] drew a clear distinction between wasteful emergency relief programs and planned public works. Bowley argued for the anticipation of necessary public work in periods of depression on the ground that the inauguration of a flexible public works program before unemployment became acute would aid general business conditions. It was calculated that if a small percentage (3 or 4 percent) of the ordinary annual public works outlays had been reserved in ordinary years and the accumulated proceeds spent in the depression period the sum would have proved sufficient to stabilize total employment during the preceding decade. This plan found expression in the Development and Road Funds Act of Great Britain in 1909. The act stated that national public works and Parliamentary grants to local authorities for local public works "must be expended having in mind the general state and prospects of employment." [14] This program was tried in subsequent years, but on a very limited scale. During the 1920-1921 recession large sums were spent for public improvements in accordance with a cyclical perspective, and the results were comparatively successful viewed in the light of previous unpremeditated expansions, although the real possibilities of a long-range program were only slightly realized.[15]

on the Pyramids served to supply the idle peasants with subsistence. J. Baikie, quoted by C. J. Bullock (*Politics, Finance and Consequences*, pp. 9-10), suggests that "Khufu's gigantic scheme was not only a selfish attempt to secure immortality for himself, but incidentally proved to be the first unemployment relief scheme on record." J. Baikie, *History of Egypt*, I, 122.

[11] Sidney and Beatrice Webb, *English Poor Law History*; Hill and Lubin, *The British Attack on Unemployment*, pp. 13-17, 237-240; National Bureau of Economic Research, *Planning and Control of Public Works*, pp. 168-169.

[12] The practical difficulties here are described in detail by R. C. Davison, "Unemployment Relief in Germany," *The Economic Journal* (London), XL (March, 1930), 140.

[13] Great Britain, Poor Law Commission, *Minority Report*, 1909, Part II.

[14] After O. T. Mallory, "The Long Range Planning of Public Works," National Bureau of Economic Research, *Business Cycles and Unemployment*, p. 237.

[15] *Ibid.*, p. 238.

One of the more serious attempts to alleviate depressed conditions by a large public works program was made in the United States in 1921–1922—the postwar depression period.[16] The President's Conference on Unemployment, held in 1921, was responsible for formulating a program representing the first centralized nation-wide attack on depression in this country. The severe unemployment situation and the recent experience with national planning in connection with the war made recourse to that type of action not unexpected.

The most important immediate result of the President's Conference was the proposal and wide adoption of the plan that local and state public construction operations be enlarged to provide employment for those without work and to stimulate private industry by creating a demand for a wide variety of raw materials. The program which resulted from the Unemployment Conference saw a record expansion of all types of public works by a majority of cities.[17] Several hundred local emergency committees followed the program drawn up at the conference to anticipate necessary public works. While the need for federal economy, peculiarly enough, was held to militate against any general expansion of federal outlay, a $75,000,000 federal grant to the states in the autumn of 1921, supplementing local expenditures, stimulated this type of activity somewhat.

Purely technical considerations, however, do not allow perfect freedom of timing. That is, for certain types of projects—say, a bridge or a dam—a fairly inflexible construction period is involved;[18] once a project is started, it is not usually feasible to suspend operations because of unexpected economic developments. A public works stabilization program is most effective in an environment experiencing more or less regular cyclical swings. Given the rigidity of actual construction periods, an erratic cyclical pattern might very well destroy the basis for a controlled flexible works program. Violent fluctuations of relatively short duration would be fatal to the success of a stabilization program.

The postponable category of public works, chiefly large-scale undertakings, should ideally reach its maximum level during the depths of the depression phase. If the depression (or recession) phase is short-

[16] Gayer, *Public Works in Prosperity and Depression*, chap. ii.
[17] See National Bureau of Economic Research, *Business Cycles and Unemployment*, pp. 242–243.
[18] United States, National Resources Planning Board, *The Economic Effects of the Federal Public Works Expenditures, 1933–1938*, chap. vi.

THE EMERGENCE OF FISCAL POLICY

lived and the projects undertaken are slow in getting started, the construction program would be expanded in a period of comparatively high economic levels. Such unfortunate timing is not likely where there are many projects which require relatively short periods for completion. Adjustment to the vagaries of the economic situation could be effected rather promptly (on the purely technical side of construction, omitting administrative complications), were public undertakings of the above type.

The downright unwieldiness of "controlled" public works may well exaggerate, as we have just indicated, the very cyclical pattern they are designed to reduce. In addition to the relative severity of business fluctuations, the uncertain duration of the various phases of the cycle raises another difficult problem. The inflexibility of heavy public works is such as to suggest that they be delayed until after the recession has been in progress for some time and there is less likelihood of a sudden reversal. There exists, however, the difficulty, in this connection, that the inauguration of public construction may be delayed until the recession is at an end and the high phase of the cycle approaching. Since many big projects, such as power dams, bridges, and so forth, require at least a year or so up to three years or more for completion, the difficulties may well be appreciated. Were it possible to reserve projects more characteristic of the routine or unpostponable category, such as ordinary repairs and replacements, usually relatively small in size and large in number, the above problem would vanish. But such is not the case. While the character of the heavy large-scale projects varies according to the governmental unit, the basic problem is in substance identical for all public administrative bodies.

The calculations upon which Bowley and Stuart based their planned public works scheme rest upon the assumption of mild variations in business activity. The period in English economic activity to which their proposals have reference (the decade 1897–1906) was characterized by comparatively slight fluctuations; the maximum decline in total wages paid out in this period was about 5 percent. It would have been possible to stabilize employment throughout this decade by the reservation of 3 or 5 percent of government orders, or about £40 million.[19] The relatively slight decline in activity in three of the ten years presented a problem eminently susceptible to the stabilization approach. Furthermore, the opportunities for public capital investment

[19] Cf. Clark, *The Economics of Planning Public Works*, pp. 9–10.

were large and varied, given the relative importance of state enterprises in the economy, and sizable expansions could have been forthcoming had the need been urgent.

PUMP-PRIMING

A somewhat different approach to public works programs was adopted by the supporters of what has come to be known as the "pump-priming" program. The pump-priming concept holds that it may be possible to inaugurate a recovery movement through the impetus provided by public expenditures. The various adjustments prerequisite to recovery can, it is contended, be speedily implemented by an expansion of public expenditures.[20]

Whether the impediments to recovery lie in the area of entreprenurial psychology, cost-price distortions, inadequate consumer demand, special problems in certain industries, or related and subsidiary problems, it is contended that the necessary adjustment can be precipitated by government action. The importance of psychological factors in the business picture is clearly recognized in addition to the more objective aspects of cyclical phenomena. There is shrewd appreciation that if businessmen can be convinced that pump-priming is a sound argument, this in itself may constitute a powerful factor in achieving an upward movement.

This approach does not recognize any fundamental and deep-seated changes in the nature of the economic system. No credence is placed in the doctrine of chronic stagnation. All the pump-priming concept comprehends is the existence of a serious depression and the absence of the necessary conditions for recovery.

Two different phases of the program may be distinguished: (1) that aspect of the program involving government outlays for public works projects, direct relief to the unemployed needy, subsidies and grants in aid to local governments, and (2) loans to financial institutions, business corporations, and partnerships, aid to distressed mortgage holders, and the like. The first part of the pump-priming program, the more direct part of the program, affects the income stream immediately by adding to the purchasing power of the nation through relief wages and outright relief grants, plus payments for purchases of materials and supplies involved in construction undertakings. In addition to the primary employment involved in public works operations,

[20] See Burns and Watson, *Government Spending and Economic Expansion*, chap. iv.

THE EMERGENCE OF FISCAL POLICY

such as the direct employment on the project and the indirect employment created by the production of the necessary materials along with the associated services involved, there is what J. M. Clark calls [21] "secondary employment." This describes the employment resulting from the expenditures made by the original recipients of income from the public works or direct relief program.

The second category of activities, the lending part of the program, helps offset the reduction of income flowing from the destruction of capital assets, bankruptcies, and so forth. The cumulative deflationary process, feeding on the inability to procure bank credit, derives from as well as aggravates the strained banking system. The extension of government loans to financial institutions and business firms aids in stemming the dash for liquidity and in reducing the rate of insolvencies. By easing the credit situation and relieving the cumulative deflationary spiral, a basis is laid for a return to an orderly credit situation so indispensable to any upward economic movement. The second, or loan portion of the program, thus helps to provide a hospitable environment for recovery. The first, or spending, portion of the program, provides the dynamic fuel for the recovery ascent.

One of the outstanding characteristics of a pump-priming program is the degree of flexibility associated with such a plan—flexibility with regard to both the size and the timing of the program. The range of activities on the spending side runs all the way from direct relief grants, subsidies to governmental subdivisions and corporate enterprises [22]—which can be made with little delay and quickly terminated —to large public works projects slow in getting into operation and requiring several years for completion. This relative freedom in scheduling public outlays contrasts with the inflexibility of a public works program of the type earlier described.

The different stages in the pump-priming process may be briefly noted. The first and second stages involve the actual spending by the government and the secondary spending by the recipients of public funds—both consumer and business spending. With the realization of the third stage, namely, the stimulation of net private investment, our pump-priming scheme has achieved its goal. This final step is the real test of a pump-priming program. If an enlarged volume of purchasing power by itself and through its secondary repercussions con-

[21] *The Economics of Planning Public Works*, p. 80.
[22] For business enterprises this form of aid more commonly takes the shape of loans.

tributes to an inauguration of private capital outlay, the pump-priming objective has been realized. Quite clearly, the volume of new investment may vary greatly—from an insignificant amount to a quantity sufficient to produce relatively full employment. Formally it is probably correct to hold that a pump-priming plan has not fulfilled its goal unless the program induces sufficient new investment to produce relatively prosperous conditions within a reasonable period.

The analysis of the secondary effects of a given volume of public expenditures upon consumption is discussed under the multiplier principle. This theoretical tool has in recent years come to assume considerable importance in studying the effectiveness of public spending as a means of securing recovery. The secondary effects of public expenditures or investment on private investment are covered by the term "relation" or, more commonly, under the "acceleration principle." This division of the problem of secondary repercussions is hardly fundamental to the problem of pump-priming, but merely represents an effort to break down the analysis of secondary effects.

THE MULTIPLIER

The opening gun in the theoretical study of the effects of government spending was R. F. Kahn's widely read article in the *Economic Journal* of June, 1931—"The Relation of Home Investment to Unemployment." Mr. Kahn traces the primary increment of government expenditure through its successive courses, showing how a portion of the income created is lost at each stage through various types of leakages, that is, savings, expenditures on imports, and a third type of subtraction for relief payments.[23] The ratio of secondary to primary employment, stemming from public works, is determined by calculating the portion of income which at each successive stage is spent on home consumption.

The Kahn "relation" was adopted with but slight alteration [24] by Keynes in his *General Theory* and plays an integral part in the theory of employment.[25] In the Keynesian analysis three all-important psy-

---

[23] For this final adjustment a deduction is made from current wages of that portion of the dole previously received by the newly employed individual, financed at the expense of saving or borrowing. This is known as the nontransfer portion of the dole.

[24] Kahn's multiplier may be called an "employment multiplier," since it measures the ratio of an increment of primary employment in the investment industries to the total employment produced. Keynes's multiplier is an investment multiplier.

[25] *General Theory*, p. 113.

THE EMERGENCE OF FISCAL POLICY

chological predispositions, unchanging for undefined "short periods," provide the basic framework responsible for determining the level of national income and the volume of employment; they are (1) the propensity to consume, (2) liquidity preference, and (3) the marginal efficiency of capital or demand for capital. Since there is no occasion to traverse the much-traveled terrain of the *General Theory*, it will suffice for present purposes merely to outline briefly the relationship among the above propensities.

Where Yw equals income in terms of wage units and Cw is the consumption in terms of wage units, $\frac{dCw}{dYw}$ is the marginal propensity to consume. The above ratio informs us how the next increment of output will be divided between consumption and savings. Since $\triangle$ Yw = $\triangle$ Cw + $\triangle$ Iw, where Cw and Iw represent increments of consumption and investment, $\triangle$ Yw = K$\triangle$I, where $1 - \frac{1}{(k)}$ is equal to the marginal propensity to consume $(c + c^2 + c^3 + \ldots = 1 - \frac{1}{k})$. The investment multiplier, k, is a ratio which "tells us that, when there is an increment of aggregate investment, income will increase by an amount which is k times the increment of investment." [26] The multiplier "establishes a precise relationship, given the propensity to consume, between aggregate employment and income and the rate of investment." [27]

The theory is designed to establish general principles by which the quantitative relationship between an increment of net investment and the resulting increment of aggregate investment and income associated with it may be estimated.

To continue with this schema: as already indicated, the marginal propensity to consume determines the division of an increment of output between consumption and investment. If the marginal propensity to consume is unity, the whole of the increment will be consumed and no savings will result. When the marginal propensity to consume is two-thirds, the marginal propensity to save is one-third. The relationship between the marginal propensity to save and the multiplier is equally simple. The multiplier is the reciprocal of the marginal propensity to save.

The multiplier, as used by Keynes, apparently refers only to secondary or induced consumption and excludes secondary investment which may possibly be induced by the increased consumption level.

[26] *Ibid.*, p. 115. [27] *Ibid.*, p. 113.

The multiplier, therefore, does not completely describe the developments following from an increase of government investment. It is only a partial explanation, having no reference to induced investment or, to use Harrod's term, the "relation" which explains the operation of the "acceleration principle." Any attempt to account fully for all the direct repercussions attendant on a change in the level of public investment must therefore involve a consideration of both of these principles—the multiplier concept and the relation principle. Analysis proceeding solely in multiplier terms results in understanding—to the extent that the relation principle is active and positive [28]—the total effects of public investment.[29] To sum up: the logical theory of the multiplier merely states the formal relationship between increments of net investment and secondary, or induced consumption. The relationship is assumed to be stable over "short periods."

Let us delay for a moment an examination of the implications of the multiplier theory and undertake in somewhat greater detail a presentation of its properties.[30] We may best illustrate the formal content of the multiplier by resorting to a few simple diagrams. The following set of diagrams illustrates the secondary repercussions attendant on increments of net public investment: [31]

We represent first the successive dwindling stages of a single, isolated expenditure; second, the effects produced by continued increments of investment, and third, the pattern produced by suddenly stopping a certain volume of repeated outlays. We assume in each case a multiplier of three (propensity to consume two-thirds and leakages of one-third, each successive expenditure being two-thirds of the pre-

---

[28] The "relation" or induced investment need not, of course, necessarily be positive. What is significant is the *net* increment of investment. If, as a result of governmental decision to extend outlays in an attempt to produce economic recovery, some private investment expenditures are discouraged, we are precluded from applying the relation or investment multiplier to the increased volume of public expenditure as a means of determining the *aggregate* effect of government expenditure. We must necessarily make our investment multiplier calculation only after examining its influence on private investment.

[29] Professor Paul A. Samuelson undertakes a union of the multiplier and relation principle in "Interactions between the Multiplier Analysis and the Principle of Acceleration," *Review of Economic Statistics*, XX (May, 1939), 75–78.

[30] For an analysis proceeding in terms of the velocity of money see Angell, *Investment and Business Cycles*, chaps. ix–x; chaps. xi is devoted to an appraisal of the Keynesian multiplier.

[31] Keynes's exposition is not strictly comparable. J. M. Clark has brought the Keynesian development and the successive stage analysis together in his above-the-line and below-the-line presentation. See his article, "An Appraisal of the Workability of Compensatory Devices," *A.E.R.*, XXIX (Supplement, March, 1939), 194–208. Keynes's treatment, however, appears to be timeless.

THE EMERGENCE OF FISCAL POLICY 17

ceding magnitude); the investment outlay in each case is assumed to be $100 millions.

CHART I

SUCCESSIVE STAGES OF INCOME PRODUCED BY A
SINGLE INVESTMENT OUTLAY

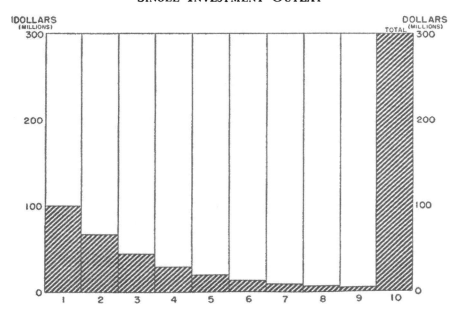

It may be seen that the successive repercussions are rapidly vitiated; the largest portion of income stimulation being realized in the first three or four stages. Column 10, which is three times as great as column 1 (k = 3), represents the summation of the primary outlay (1) and the successive repercussions (2–9).[32] In the event of a lower multiplier, the effects largely disappear in an even shorter time—from two to three stages with a multiplier of two (namely, $1 + \frac{1}{2} + \frac{1}{4} + \frac{1}{8} + \frac{1}{16}$, and so forth). If we follow Professor J. M. Clark's assumption of a two-month cycle (or "marginal multiplier time interval," after Hansen),[33]

[32] After J. M. Clark, cf. *The Economics of Planning Public Works*, p. 91.
[33] Professor Hansen distinguishes between the average and the marginal time intervals with regard to the income velocity period and the multiplier period. "The marginal income velocity refers to the velocity of the last increment of money injected into the system, and this might be higher or lower than the average velocity. . . . The marginal Multiplier period, however, refers to the time interval of the new increment of consumption expenditures flowing from the initial outlay, and this might vary for many

18   THE EMERGENCE OF FISCAL POLICY

the consumption repercussions will be almost entirely realized within four or six months after the investment outlay (with a multiplier of 2).

Let us consider the pattern produced by repeated government investment outlays. With expenditures continued over a period of time the expansive effect would be determined in the same manner as was the outcome of a single increment; the original expenditure plus the successive installments and their repercussions. The following diagram is based on the assumptions made in connection with Chart I (that is, Multiplier of 3, constant rate of leakages, an investment outlay of $100 millions in each case, and so forth). Other relevant factors are regarded as unaffected.

CHART II

SUCCESSIVE STAGES OF INCOME PRODUCED BY
CONTINUED INVESTMENT OUTLAYS

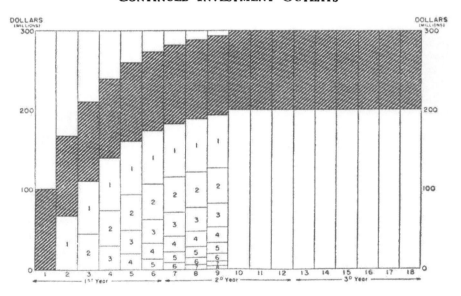

reasons (particularly the economic groups affected) considerably from the average time interval for consumption expenditures." Professor Hansen also clearly distinguishes between the average time interval between successive consumption expenditures (which is the subject of our investigation) and the average time interval involved in the income velocity of money. The circuit velocity of money refers to the average time involved in the exchange of a dollar from one individual to another. This is quite different from the Multiplier time interval which "is the average interval between successive consumption expenditures." *Fiscal Policy and Business Cycles*, p. 270.

THE EMERGENCE OF FISCAL POLICY

The above diagram traces both the building up of the cumulative effects of expenditures through repeated outlays plus the diminishing repercussions attending each individual expenditure. The effects of continued government outlays exert their full force after about nine periods; thereafter, continued doses of government investment will serve only to maintain the previous level of income, not to increase it. The smaller the portion lost by leakage or, to put it another way, the higher the multiplier, the later the asymptote will be reached.

From the investment of the first six periods, totaling $600 millions, there will result induced income (on the basis of a multiplier of 3) amounting in all the successive stages—until the repercussions disappear—to $1,200 millions or twice the initial expenditure. The following diagram indicates the manner in which expenditures will taper off.

Chart III

Successive Stages of Income Produced by Six Investment Outlays

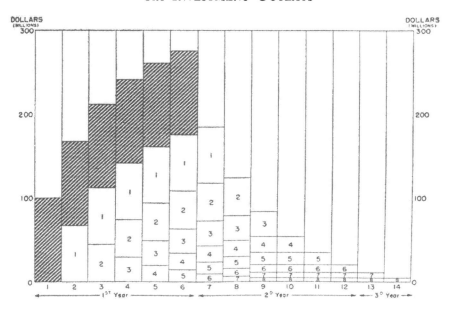

The preceding diagram shows that a sudden cessation of government outlays will be very quickly reflected in a diminution of income.

Assuming that each bar represents a period of two months, the largest portion of induced consumption will disappear two or three stages subsequent to the discontinuance of government investment. This point has been made much of by those who oppose expansion of government expenditures on the ground that these outlays are self-perpetuating in the sense that they must be continued or else the national income will quickly return to the level prevailing before their introduction. This interpretation is, however, a crude one, derived from a static formulation such as that presented above. It assumes all other independent and related factors which enter into a determination of the national income have not been altered as a result of the additional volume of investment.

The foregoing diagrams indicate how the successive income stages behave in time. The formal, mechanical structure of the "logical" multiplier involving constant leakages and elimination of all lags is seen to be a schema which requires considerable modification if applied to the real world. Keynes, however, when stepping down from the "logical" theory of the multiplier to the actual relationships in a dynamic economy does not oblige us by suggesting the necessary amendments, even though he claims, in a later section, that the multiplier may help in an analysis of the "phenomena of the cycle." [34]

The multiplier merely expresses the total result of a net increment of investment as a multiple of that addition, that is, it represents merely an arithmetic relationship. The problem, however, is not one of aggregates, but one of *significant relationships.* That is to say, the meaningful criterion is not so much the hypothecated numerical product flowing from a net addition, but rather the economic consequences of this addition. We may conceive of an "area of inconsequence" in national government expenditures where changes upward or downward of several or tens of millions of dollars in any month may be quickly absorbed in increased idle balances, decreased inventories, debt reduction [35] and so forth, from which no significant alteration of the general economic situation will ensue. The volume of the net addition is of crucial importance. Keynes, it appears, is on the wrong track when he states that "in any case, the multiplier is likely to be greater for a small net increment of investment than for a large incre-

---

[34] *General Theory,* p. 313.
[35] There is a distinction between hoarding and repayment of debt. The latter may result in stimulating activity while the former is always deflationary.

THE EMERGENCE OF FISCAL POLICY

ment; so that, where substantial changes are in view, we must be guided by the average value of the multiplier based on the average propensity to consume over the range in question." [36] While this may very well be true, it is not the really important issue.[37]

Let us suppose that a small net addition of investment, say $2 million, is in the course of several circuits multiplied five or ten times and produces $10 or $20 millions of national income. While we may be duly impressed with this happy phenomenon, we may posit the question of the significance of this change in relation to the aggregate flow of national income. We must conclude that it is inconsequential. Total employment opportunities will not have been materially affected. The multiplier is no aid in determining whether or not a particular net increment has had a significant effect on the cycle and national income. While Keynes in his comments on the economic situation of the United States and Great Britain describes changes in the importance of public outlays as a fraction of total national income, this order of analysis, the writer believes, does not stem from his formal presentation of the multiplier, but instead represents no more than a "scientific guess." [38]

Keynes in his visit to this country in the spring of 1934 made some interesting estimates of the consequences of various changes in federal expenditures. He estimated that if aggregate federal emergency expenditures fell to $200 millions a month we would experience a decline in economic activity. Were we to spend $400 million a month, however, Keynes claimed we would promote a strong recovery movement.[39] This type of statement while possibly entirely correct at the time, is hardly derived from the multiplier concept. Rather it would seem to be based upon an appraisal of the various factors operative in the current business picture, such as prices, profits, expectations, the condition of inventories, need for replacements, business confidence, and a host of other strategic factors in the economic situation,

---

[36] *General Theory*, p. 121.

[37] For an enlightened discussion of the importance of the size of government outlays in relation to business behavior see Burns and Watson, *Government Spending and Economic Expansion*, chap. vii.

[38] See J. W. Angell's critique of the Keynesian multiplier, *Investment and Business Cycles*, chap. xi.

[39] Keynes believed we would enjoy a high multiplier. "Four hundred million dollars monthly is not much more than 11 per cent of the national income; yet it may, directly and indirectly, increase the national income by at least three or four times this amount." *New York Times*, June 10, 1934.

all of which do not properly fall into the domain of Keynes's "static" multiplier.[40]

PUMP-PRIMING (CONTINUED)

The success of the pump-priming plan will depend upon (1) induced consumption and (2) induced investment resulting from the original public outlays.

The necessary expansion of employment and payrolls involved will, it is held, further augment the demand for consumers' goods. The additional activity in the consumers' goods industries will produce a demand for renewals and perhaps some new plant. The latter is less probable, since it is hardly likely that operations are being conducted at a point close to capacity output. Such demand for additional plant and equipment as may ensue, will soon taper off unless consumer demand *continues* to rise to higher and higher levels. The multiplier effects peter out in time. In the absence of continued expansion of demand in the consumers' goods industries, the output of investment goods is restricted to mere replacement and modernization requirements.[41] It is consequently contended that a recovery based on a revival of consumer purchasing can proceed "no farther than it is pushed. It has no momentum of its own. It has no inner power to complete its own development." [42] The second part of this picture, the stimulus of the capital goods industries through government orders, presents a somewhat more encouraging outlook. Increased activity in the durable goods industries will directly affect the area most severely hit by the depression; this is the sector of the economy which undergoes the most violent fluctuations.

Economic prosperity characteristically finds expression through enlargement of plant capacity. This expansion, Hansen claims, is not geared to the volume of consumption demand, but is determined largely by technological innovation and business expectations. Consumption levels are determined in large part by the behavior of the capital goods industries, not vice versa. To return to our present problem: The measure of the effect of government orders upon the capital goods industries will be a function largely of (1) the size of government purchases and (2) the coefficient of acceleration. No appreci-

[40] The multiplier as developed by J. M. Clark, however, can be interpreted dynamically. See Angell's discussion, *Investment and Business Cycles*, p. 195.
[41] Hansen, *Full Recovery or Stagnation*, chap. xvii.
[42] *Ibid.*, p. 282.

THE EMERGENCE OF FISCAL POLICY

able volume of new net investment is likely to result in a situation characterized by low utilization of existing plant capacity unless stimulated by outstanding technological development.

New investment may be generated as a consequence of a moderate revival in the capital goods industries, since a recovery here may provide the necessary spark of confidence prerequisite to recovery. Business may be bogged down in the depths of despondency, profit margins may be very low, and so forth. There may be on hand a considerable variety of new investment opportunities which are being neglected until an apparently more propitious time. The optimism engendered by a recovery in the key capital goods industries may give the "go" signal to the installation of new and improved technological innovations, new products, and devices. In the event that the recovery from depression has been delayed, not because of any fundamental structural, or secular developments, but because of psychological features, lack of confidence, and so forth—then government stimulus to the capital goods industries might set the ball rolling. In time the acceleration principle may become operative. If, however, none of these dynamic features are present, there is no reason to expect any significantly greater repercussions in this area than that which could be expected to occur in the consumer goods field. It should be pointed out, however, that it might be possible for a rise in demand for consumer goods to effect some of these same changes.

How is the pump-priming program to be financed? Any financial program which merely alters the direction of the flow of investment funds rather than increasing the volume of consumption and investment would be self-defeating. The contradiction involved in financing a spending program through taxes resting largely on consumption is too apparent to require comment. The adoption of regressive taxation may be a useful device for reducing or eliminating budgetary deficits, but would clearly operate to cancel out the stimulative effects of government spending.[43]

The pump-priming program as interpreted by the author ideally calls for a cyclical budgetary balance.[44] This plan is designed to forestall any long-run increase in outstanding debt. Deficits realized in depression years are to be offset by the surplus revenue enjoyed in prosperous years. The implications of a cyclical budget will be examined later in this chapter.

[43] See Chapter VI for a discussion of various aspects of taxation policy.
[44] See Burns and Watson, *Government Spending and Economic Expansion*, p. 46.

At what point in the depression should resort be had to the public spending program: (1) at the outset of the depression; (2) during the lowest ebb of business activity, or (3) after a recovery movement is already under way—after the worst is over? The theory of pump-priming, unfortunately, has not expressed a clear view on this very important issue. What are the criteria to be examined before this decision can be made? It is, of course, not true that the theory of pump-priming has left us in the dark with regard to these crucial issues, but the answers to these problems are incompletely developed.[45] What follows is an attempt to develop this aspect of the theory of pump-priming—consistent with its major assumptions.

While we have spoken thus far of pump-priming programs as though there existed but one precise and unambiguous species, we suggest that there more properly may be described a whole range of such programs, all bearing the same title, stretching from the very timorous and economizing type, which would throw crumbs into the hungry maw of depression, to the aggressive variant, committed to the policy of buying recovery "at any price."[46] Policies of timing, volume, and duration of public spending will vary, therefore, according to the character of the particular program; the matter of *intent* or conviction of the feasibility of spending as a recovery measure can best be measured by the type of program actually agreed upon and executed.

The decision as to the timing and type of public expenditures rests, first of all, upon an analysis of the character of the depression maladjustments; secondly, upon belief in the efficacy of pump-priming as a recovery expedient; thirdly, upon an appraisal of the general economic and political environment. We have no need to dwell upon the existence of secular-stagnation, for the pump-priming theory assumes essentially temporary maladjustments. Is it necessary to delay action until the maladjustments have begun to effect their own cure, or is it true that there exists no such need for initial self-correction?

More concretely, if we envisage a depression arising essentially from an unbalance in the price structure, should the government take immediate steps to expand expenditures to prevent a decline? Is there a danger that such action may prolong an untenable price situation? Should pump-priming be postponed until a "natural" correction has begun with its assurance of a more healthy state of affairs? Are the

---

[45] See Samuelson, "The Theory of Pump-Priming Reexamined," *American Economic Review*, XXX (September, 1940), 492–506.
[46] See J. M. Keynes, *The Means to Prosperity*.

THE EMERGENCE OF FISCAL POLICY

expenditures required by an early government response disproportionate to the results achieved? The relative costs, of course, cannot be calculated but the differences involved would no doubt be very great. The final decision will depend on the different weights attributed to the social consequences of a lengthier depression, the expenditures entailed and the belief in the efficacy of the general policy of government pump-priming.

The pursuance of a "hands off" government policy in expectation of a "normal adjustment" suggests confidence in some type of inevitable correction. The belief expressed by Professor Slichter [47] that government spending should be delayed until the bottom of the depression has been reached seems only a milder form of the view that a depression is primarily a healthy purgative, performing a useful and necessary function—an opinion which appears to have lost many of its supporters in the last decade.[48] Mr. Samuelson,[49] on the other hand, remarks that it is not good policy for us to let business deteriorate in order to give it an opportunity to get well again. He calls for nipping any incipient deflation in the bud.

Any general proposition, however, which states that public spending should be inaugurated at a particular stage of the downturn begs the basic issue—which is the determination of the factors responsible for the downturn. If the recession has been precipitated by serious cost-price disparities, price maladjustments, artificially inflated or unsupportable price levels, abnormally high inventories in key industries, adverse legislation affecting profits outlook, threatening foreign situation, and so forth, it is not likely that a prompt governmental spending response will be effective in reversing the cyclical swing. Pump-priming under such conditions seems distinctly unpromising. For the conditions earlier described (on pages 12, 23) where new investment may be encouraged along with an improved business psychology, an early pump-priming program appears desirable. Under the conditions indicated, a prompt inauguration of public outlays may overcome the prevalent inertia.

Mr. Samuelson's concern lest the deflationary spiral be permitted to proceed so far that a reversal of the movement becomes vastly more

---

[47] "The Economics of Public Works," *American Economic Review*, XXIV (March, 1934), 174–185.

[48] Professor Hansen, for example, who expressed such a view in his *Economic Stabilization in an Unbalanced World*, has since altered his position.

[49] "The Theory of Pump-Priming Reexamined," *American Economic Review*, XXX (September, 1940), 492–506.

difficult is quite realistic. Certainly our experience between 1930 and 1933 justifies this apprehension. However, it does not follow that pump-priming outlays should follow promptly after the outset of a cyclical downturn. The adoption of this orientation signifies, in effect, the belief that the economic situation at the prosperity phase, prior to the downturn, was a satisfactory one. The explanation of the decline is consequently made somewhat difficult unless the presence of additional new factors can be established.

The specific point in the recession selected for the inauguration of a pump-priming program should depend, as suggested above, upon the whole array of circumstances giving shape to the cycle. While the danger of delaying action beyond the time that such response is likely to be most effective is always present, so too is the danger of prolonging various cyclical maladjustments through too prompt a response.

The strategic timing of a pump-priming program as described above is valid only in reference to an economy alternating between prosperity and depression stages of roughly comparable duration. If fluctuations occur about a norm of depression or if prosperity periods are of the briefest duration and depressions of extended length, then we are in an environment not amenable to a pump-priming program.

The pump-priming theory rests upon the idea that the government at some point or other will be able to withdraw its support as a contributor to the income stream without initiating a downturn. Such a move is clearly possible only when the level of economic activity is rising. Government net-income-creating expenditures are expected to generate secondary repercussions conducive to getting the economy out of its sluggish mire. How far recovery will proceed cannot, of course, be calculated beforehand; it will be determined by the volume of expenditures, the size of the multiplier, and the extent to which the acceleration principle is operative. On the other hand it will be affected by factors in the economic situation quite independent of government action. Full recovery may be achieved, or something well below that level.

At what point in the upward movement should government pump-priming outlays begin to taper off? At what level should they be completely withdrawn? In the case of a pump-priming program involving in large part the construction of heavy public works projects there is the difficulty of curtailing such projects; we shall exclude this complication, having already touched upon it.

THE EMERGENCE OF FISCAL POLICY 27

There is, of course, no patent answer as to when government net contributory spending should terminate or taper off. The negative maxim that government outlays should not be reduced if such a move is likely to precipitate an economic decline is hardly a sufficient basis for action, although it does represent a starting point for arriving at some decision. The pressure to achieve a cyclical budgetary balance must be weighed against the danger of terminating the recovery movement. The problem of measuring the strength of recovery forces at various stages of revival, independent of the influence of government stimulus is clearly a complicated one. Any conclusions reached may be of questionable validity. The frequent reversals of spending policy in the United States between 1933 and 1938 are testimony to the difficulties of forecasting in this sphere. The relative responsibility of a reduction in federal net contributory outlay as a causal factor in the 1937 recession has been hotly contested. The multiplicity of factors operative in any given economic situation trace so intricate a design that only fairly general relationships can be established among the data. Methods being developed by Tinbergen [50] and Lundberg [51] for dealing precisely with the independent variables responsible for cyclical fluctuations are suggestive, but hardly capable of supplying the desired answers.[52]

From the spending side of the pump-priming program it would seem that retrenchment should be delayed until the realization of a business level close to full employment. As long as there exists any appreciable amount of unutilized resources, spending should be continued. But this precept ignores the necessity of meeting previously incurred deficits. This obligation may require that net contributory expenditures be discontinued with the *entrance* of the economy into the "prosperity phase" of the cycle, despite the risk that such a decision may very well jeopardize the continuance of the recovery movement. The danger of nipping an incipient recovery in the bud is clearly present here.[53] This chance will have to be taken, however, if the cyclical balancing plan is rigorously followed.

This conflict between budgetary considerations on the one hand and the spending objectives of the pump-priming program on the

[50] Tinbergen, *Statistical Testing of Business Cycle Theories, 1.*
[51] Lundberg, *Studies in the Theory of Economic Expansion.*
[52] See Keynes's review of Tinbergen's volume in *Economic Journal*, XLIX (September, 1939), 558–568.
[53] It should be noted on the other hand that a deflationary fiscal policy may be necessary to keep a recovery from developing into a mere price boom at full employment.

other cannot be avoided in any program envisaging a cyclical balance. While it is true that there exists a range of discretion in regard to the precise point at which retrenchment should begin, this freedom is limited. Although there is no specific limit governing the total volume of pump-priming outlays similar to that involved in the public works stabilization program, some rough limit does exist based upon an estimate of surpluses in the anticipated prosperity period.

We can see from the above discussion the nature of the restrictions imposed upon the spending program because of the requirement of a cyclical budgetary balance. As the writer has defined the pump-priming program, such a balance is necessary. If the limitations imposed in this manner on government spending are deemed inimical to the achievement of recovery, then these restrictions may presumably have to be altered.

We have, of course, simplified various aspects of the pump-priming program. Numerous factors prevent unrestricted changes in the level of expenditures. In addition to the engineering aspects of the program described above, there is the difficulty of curtailing expenditures in good years. People receiving direct relief and those employed on works projects can safely be thrown on the labor market only if there is assurance that industry can rapidly absorb them. The absorption process may be slow, and the recovery may halt at a point well below full employment. Once certain social and economic responsibilities have been accepted, they cannot be freely discarded. The extent to which such social pressure will find political expression cannot be known in advance, but its existence, in some measure, can be taken for granted.

We shall not carry this analysis further, since we shall return to it in subsequent pages. For the present, it is necessary to appreciate that various political and social considerations may limit the freedom of decision on purely economic grounds. This is true, of course, of every economic decision, but it is of special importance in programs which require complete freedom of timing for their successful conduct.

III. COMPENSATORY PUBLIC SPENDING AND SECULAR-STAGNATION

UNLIKE the preceding types of government spending theory designed for an economy characterized by more or less regular cyclical fluctuations, the present approach is oriented toward the longer-run problem of chronic depression, or secular-stagnation—to use the term popularized by Professor Hansen. The stagnation theory attempts to explain the depression of the thirties in terms of basic and deep-seated changes in our economic environment. The problem of our generation is held to be that of idle "savings" attributable to (1) a deficiency of mass purchasing power and (2) a deficiency of private investment outlets. The problem of idle funds, or oversaving, can be described as a situation in which the *savings* out of the income from immediate *past* production exceed investment in products of current production.[1]

One of the cornerstones in classical economic theory has been the doctrine that the restricted supply of capital accumulated out of savings constituted the greatest restraint upon the limits of economic expansion.[2] The rate of capital accumulation, it was held, governed the rate of economic expansion. There could not, therefore, possibly exist a condition of oversaving (in the above sense of the term). In the period in which this theory first appeared, the shortage of capital was all too apparent. Although the "shortage of capital" school was the dominant theoretical group throughout the whole of the nineteenth century, it did not go undisputed. A small dissenting group early made its appearance. This school contended, contrary to the classicists, that the core of our economic ills could be traced to a deficiency of purchasing power relative to productive capacity.[3] Savings,

[1] See Clark, "An Appraisal of the Workability of Compensatory Devices," *American Economic Review*, XXIX (Supplement, March, 1939), p. 205.

[2] Adam Smith stressed the idea that the limited supply of capital established definite limitations on the growth of production and employment. The famous formula that "industry is limited by capital" was derived from Smith's writings. See Gourvitch, *Survey of Economic Theory on Technological Change and Employment*, pp. 33–38.

[3] The underconsumption or oversaving theory of the business cycle maintained by this group has a very long although hardly revered history. Regarded as heretical in its earlier period when it found supporters in such men as Lord Lauderdale, Malthus, and Siamondi, in recent years, with various modifications, it has been more scientifically re-

it was held, could not be certain of employment, since there existed a tendency for savings to become superfluous, not because of lack of desire for larger volume of production, but because of a deficiency of *effective* demand. Saving was undertaken by a few, while deficiencies in purchasing power were a mass phenomenon.

Keynes's writings have done much to popularize the underconsumption theory in recent years. While not primarily an advocate of the underconsumption thesis, Keynes gives allegiance to this approach in many passages of his *General Theory*.[4] Haberler thinks that Keynes's underconsumptionist, oversaving approach applies primarily "to depressions of longer duration."[5] This would seem to be somewhat inaccurate, however, since Keynes makes it quite clear that any recession or depression may be produced because the propensity to save (of certain groups in society) increases. While the emphasis has shifted somewhat and the analysis has been refined considerably, the basic approach of the underconsumption theorists remains.

The oversavings theory of the cycle has gained considerable support in government circles in the last decade or so. The argument is advanced that a deficiency of consumer purchasing power was primarily responsible for the depression of 1929-1933 and our failure to realize prosperity in the subsequent years.

Since the dependence of the stagnation school upon the more modern formulations of the underconsumptionist theorists is frequently not made clear, we shall take occasion here to go beyond this brief introduction and present a résumé of that analysis.

It is, perhaps, incorrect to refer to the "underconsumptionist theory of the cycle" because, properly speaking, it represents an analysis of only one phase of the cycle—the depression phase; no explanation of the behavior of the entire cycle is provided. The more recent developments of the underconsumption theory borrow numerous features from the monetary and overinvestment theories of the cycle.

Oversaving is a phenomenon attributable to the inequalities in the distribution of wealth and income. Abundant statistical evidence exists as to the nature of this concentration. Keynes regards this inequality of income distribution (making for appreciable differences in the "propensity to consume") as partially responsible for depression ex-

stated by J. A. Hobson, Major C. H. Douglas, Messrs. W. T. Foster and W. Catchings, and others.

[4] Haberler, *Prosperity and Depression*, 1939 ed., p. 233.   [5] *Ibid.*, p. 234.

SECULAR-STAGNATION

cesses. The consumption expenditures of the entire community would expand if differences in income were reduced or eliminated.

The mere act of saving is, of course, not in itself injurious. If outlets exist for new investment, savings will be the source of an enlarged productive capacity and national income. If savings out of the income from past production are in excess of current investment at a point below full employment, additional saving is likely to contribute to the momentum of the decline. That is, a decrease in the demand for goods will take place because of the accumulation of hoards, idle deposits, and the liquidation of bank credit.

Foster and Catchings summarize the views of the underconsumption school.

> Progress toward greater total production [they declare] is retarded because consumer buying does not keep pace with production. Consumer buying lags behind for two reasons: first, because industry does not disburse to consumers enough money to buy the goods produced; second, because consumers, under the necessity of saving, cannot spend even as much money as they receive. There is not an even flow of money from producer to consumer, and from consumer back to producer. The expansion of the volume of money does not fully make up the deficit, for money is expanded mainly to facilitate the production of goods, and the goods must be sold to consumers for more money than the expansion has provided. Furthermore, the savings of corporations and individuals are not used to purchase the goods already in the markets, but to bring about the production of more goods. . . . Inadequacy of consumer income is, therefore, the main reason why we do not long continue to produce the wealth which natural resources, capital facilities, improvements in the arts, and the self-interest of employers and employees would otherwise enable us to produce. Chiefly because of shortage of consumer demand, both capital and labor restrict output, and nations engage in those struggles for outside markets and spheres of commercial influence which are the chief causes of war.[6]

MR. KEYNES AND UNEMPLOYMENT

We turn now to Mr. Keynes's *General Theory*, to examine some aspects of his analytical system—a system concerned with longer-run or secular considerations as well as cyclical problems. Of the three psychological propensities, (1) liquidity-preference, (2) marginal efficiency of capital, and (3) propensity to consume, which, together with the quantity of money, determine the level of employment and income, the third factor is accorded chief significance. Unemployment

[6] *Profits*, pp. 409–410.

may result from the action of any of the three propensities: (1) Liquidity preference may rise, (2) the marginal efficiency of capital may drop, or (3) the propensity to consume may decline. An equilibrium condition may very well exist at a level of activity below full employment, a position contrary to that entertained by classical economic theory, because of the insufficiency of effective demand.[7] The level of income and employment can be determined if we possess knowledge of the marginal propensity to consume, the marginal efficiency schedules of capital plus the rate of interest (liquidity preference plus the quantity of money).

We may now inquire into the considerations determining the longer-run movements of national income and employment, purely cyclical phenomena aside. The answer, following Keynes, for technologically advanced and wealthy countries like England and the United States, is to be found in the disposition of the propensity to consume to decline or, to put it in another form, the propensity to save to rise. With the accumulation of wealth, a decreasing portion of a community's funds are directed into consumption channels. The volume of savings is consequently enlarged.

Moreover, the richer the community, the wider will tend to be the gap between its actual and potential production; and therefore the more obvious and outrageous the defects of the economic system. For a poor community will be prone to consume by far the greater part of its output, so that a very modest measure of investment will be sufficient to provide full employment; whereas a wealthy community will have to discover much ampler opportunities for investment if the saving propensities of its wealthier members are to be compatible with the employment of its poorer members. . . . But worse still. Not only is the marginal propensity to consume weaker in a wealthy community, but, owing to its accumulation of capital being already larger, the opportunities for further investment are less attractive unless the rate of interest falls at a sufficiently rapid rate.[8]

Employment can rise only in the event of an increase in investment, unless there takes place an increase in the propensity to consume. It should be appreciated that while "employment is a function of the expected consumption and the expected investment, consumption is, *cet. par.*, a function of net income, i.e., of net investment (net income

---

[7] "The insufficiency of effective demand will inhibit the progress of production in spite of the fact that the marginal product of labor still exceeds in value the marginal disutility of employment." *General Theory of Employment, Interest and Money*, p. 31.

[8] *Ibid.*, p. 31.

SECULAR-STAGNATION

being equal to consumption plus net investment)."[9] Aggregate demand is the ultimate force determining the size of employment opportunities, whether the demand arises from present consumption needs or from the current anticipation of future demand. The greater, consequently, our provision for the consumption demand of the future (creation of capital goods), the less room exists for further activity in this direction and the more dependent we become upon current consumption as a source of demand. The larger our incomes, the greater the possible difference between income and consumption outlay and, by the same token, the greater the disproportionality of productive capacity to effective demand.[10] This line of analysis, although approached in a somewhat different vocabulary, has already been advanced in the underconsumption, oversaving formulations of Aftalion and others. Only in the event that future consumption demands are expected to rise, will current new capital investment take place in excess of current capital disinvestment.[11] "Every weakening in the propensity to consume regarded as a permanent habit must weaken the demand for capital as well as the demand for consumption."[12]

So far has the accumulation of wealth and the expansion of the capital goods industries progressed according to Keynes that

> a properly run community equipped with modern technical resources, of which the population is not increasing rapidly, ought to be able to bring down the marginal efficiency of capital in equilibrium approximately to zero within a single generation; so that we should attain the conditions of a quasi-stationary community where change and progress would result only from changes in technic, taste, population and institutions with the products of capital selling at a price proportioned to labor, etc., embodied in them on just the same principles as govern the prices of consumption—goods into which capital charges enter in an insignificant degree.[13]

Mr. Keynes prescribes as an antidote to the above condition (1) tax measures to decrease the propensity to save, and (2) the creation of outlets for new investment through public capital investment, financed by borrowing.

Mr. Keynes has not undertaken any detailed analysis of the particular features of contemporary capitalism which differentiates it from the previous era of rapid expansion. The theoretical system designed by Keynes is primarily an analytical machine to facilitate investigation of a number of cyclical and secular problems. The particular conclu-

[9] *Ibid.*, p. 98.   [10] *Ibid.*, pp. 104–105.   [11] *Ibid.*, p. 105.
[12] *Ibid.*, p. 106.   [13] *Ibid.*, pp. 220–221.

sions and recommendations for public policy arrived at rest, for the most part, upon a generalized description of the economic world rather than on detailed institutional investigation. We shall attempt to present a brief synthesis of the views of Professor Hansen and others into the nature of the secular structural changes of the last few decades by way of evaluating Keynes's analysis and the secular-stagnation doctrine.[14]

MR. HANSEN AND SECULAR-STAGNATION

The secular-stagnation doctrine, as developed by Professor Hansen, stems directly from the economic-progress theories of Wicksell,[15] Cassel,[16] Spiethoff,[17] Tugan-Baranowski,[18] and (to a lesser degree) Schumpeter.[19] No significant extension of the role performed by technological progress is attempted. Instead, Hansen presents a synthesis of the underconsumption, oversaving theories with the economic-progress theories of the foregoing writers.[20] The remote contingency described by Wicksell and Cassel—the cessation of growth—has finally materialized, according to Mr. Hansen and his group.

It was characteristic of the economists of the nineteenth century and the first three decades of the twentieth century to give scant attention to a possible cessation of economic progress.[21] The nineteenth century was par excellence a period of rapid expansion. The introduction of such inventions as the railroad, the exploitation of new foreign markets, the development of backward areas, and the expansion necessitated by growing populations required many decades of gestation. So great were the outlets for profitable investment that it seemed, per-

[14] There is not available any single exhaustive empirical study supporting the theoretical position here advanced, although evidence relating to the main contentions such as population growth, rise of new industries, and so forth, is offered. Professor A. H. Hansen has assumed the leadership in the presentation of this position. See *Full Recovery or Stagnation?* his article "Progress and Declining Population," in the *American Economic Review*, XXIX (March, 1939), 1–15, and his recent volume *Fiscal Policy and Business Cycles*. The National Resources Planning Board and the Temporary National Economic Committee have marshaled an extensive library of data and analysis bearing upon structural economic change. See also Colm and Lehmann, *Economic Consequences of Recent American Tax Policy*.

[15] *Lectures on Political Economy*, see especially pp. 211–212.
[16] *The Theory of Social Economy*, II, 620 ff.
[17] "Krisen," in *Handworterbuch der Staatswissenschaften*, 4th ed., 1925, Vol. VI.
[18] *Les Crises industrielles en Angleterre*.
[19] See his *Theory of Economic Development and Business Cycles*.
[20] Spiethoff and Cassel specifically denied the possibility that a depression may occur because of a deficiency of purchasing power or the accumulation of excessive savings.
[21] For a historical survey of the literature in the field see Alexander Gourvitch, *Survey of Economic Theory on Technological Change and Employment*, chaps. ii–iv.

haps, unreasonable to consider the likelihood of any exhaustion of such opportunities.

It is the contention of the secular-stagnation school that the long period of growth based upon capital-absorbing innovations for an expanding market has probably come to an end.[22] Our arrival at this stage of relative economic maturity, given our existing institutional organization, is interpreted to mean protracted depressed economic levels (rather than Mill's more optimistic stationary state). Cessation of growth presents the threat of prolonged declines due to the application of the acceleration principle in reverse.

Professor Hansen stresses the fact that the era in the United States between the Civil War and the World War I was one of furious growth, of greatly enlarged markets and productive capacity. The frontier was everywhere in retreat before an expanding industrialism. The transformation from a predominantly agricultural country to a highly industrialized one, capable not only of supplying internal requirements for manufactured products but also catering to a world-wide market, involved this nation in intensive activity for more than fifty years.

The rise of industrial capitalism created an environment most favorable for venture capital. The prospects of great profits in relatively uncrowded markets provided the incentive to innovators. The expectations and hopes of business during that half century, even though wildly optimistic, did not run much ahead of the actual advance of the period. Although great corporations were fairly numerous, they were primarily organized in such lines as railroads and petroleum, rather than in manufacturing. Freedom of entry, that all-important ingredient of a successful competitive system, was a reality for the most part.

The enormous expansion of population in this country, according to Hansen, accounted for roughly 60 percent of the total volume of capital formation.[23] This is particularly true of those lines of capital formation relating to population movements, that is, residential construction, various public utilities, and the production of durable as well as nondurable consumer goods. The growth of population also entailed the introduction of large-scale economies. In this perspective, population growth may be credited as responsible for a per capita increase in real income—contributing in this manner to an increase

[22] See Hansen, "Progress and Declining Population," *American Economic Review*, XXIX, No. 1 (March, 1939), 1–15.
[23] *Ibid.*, p. 8.

in capital formation. The close relationship exhibited in the past between population growth, capital formation, and aggregate output is adduced as clear proof that once this source of expansion is lost, our economy will no longer be pushed to progressively higher income levels. When the stimulus to demand attributable to rapid population growth has disappeared, only a corresponding rise in capital formation resulting from technological innovation, new industries comparable in magnitude to the automotive industry, the deepening of capital or enlarged opportunities for foreign investment will serve to compensate. Any development, moreover, which contributed to increasing per capita consumption would, in effect, be equivalent to an increase in population.

COMPENSATORY PUBLIC SPENDING

We turn now to a discussion of the scope of fiscal policy in the secular-stagnation theory. The advocacy of government outlays as a means of countering the alleged long-run tendency on the part of our economy to operate at levels well below full employment is supported by the simple stagnation thesis, which can be reduced to the following: Since there has been manifest a secular decline in private investment opportunities and since the level of income is a function of the volume of investment, it is necessary that government outlays be made to compensate for the deficiency of private investment.[24] Government outlays for capital and noncapital goods and services will be directed primarily into noncompetitive areas where increased activity may favorably affect the private sector of the economy. As has already been observed, the criteria guiding compensatory spending policy are *not* based upon the conviction that a temporary acceleration of public outlays will generate a recovery of sufficient proportions to permit reduction of government investment, although this factor may actually be operative in some measure. Rather, they rest upon the acceptance of the idea that government participation must be considered as a *continuing* activity to counterbalance the long-run deficiency of private net capital formation.

It is not possible to posit any general relationship between public and private investment activity. That ratio will be determined, generally speaking, by the state of activity in the "private" area of the

[24] In the following discussion we have not restricted our analysis to the specific recommendations of the stagnation group, but have pressed on to some of the implications of this position.

economy. It is not contrary, however, to the logic of compensatory spending theory that the public sector should at some time become dominant, but this possibility is viewed as somewhat far removed. The strategic importance of abstention from competition with private enterprise may well vanish in time, and it may become equally advisable to take over various segments of the private area where, to adopt Pigou's terminology, there exists a considerable disparity between the "net marginal *private* utility" and the "net marginal *social* utility."

The problem of timing public outlays in accordance with changes in the volume of private investment alters substantially with the growth of the relative proportion of the economy encompassed by the public sector. While the volume of public investment and non-capital expenditures currently undertaken may, within certain limits, be adjusted to the level of private activity, there exists less flexibility with regard to the provision of such regular facilities as public utilities (if the government is deeply committed in this field); in this event fluctuations in public investment will tend to move in the same direction as private investment. Government expenditures for consumers' goods and services such as medical attention, education, and so forth, are likely to become institutionalized and hence not susceptible to cyclical timing.[25]

As has been stated above, government outlays will have to be raised to levels above those prevailing in recent prewar years—expanded sufficiently to compensate for the long-run decline in the volume of private investment as well as adjusted to cyclical fluctuations which presumably will still be with us. The goal of compensatory spending like the goal of the pump-priming program is the achievement of a high level of national income or, more rigorously pursued, the realization of "full employment." In the very nature of the problem the required volume of public outlays cannot be determined in advance. In the short run, however, such calculations are liable to less error than for longer-range estimates. Such decisions will obviously have to rely upon the experience derived from actual trial and error. The complexity of causal factors contributing to the shaping of longer-run developments as well as the shorter-term business fluctuations are so great that no compensatory program can reasonably aspire to full

[25] For a discussion of consumer subsidies see Wright, *The Creation of Purchasing Power*, pp. 162–175, 196–206.

employment. We need not dwell upon the impossibility of precise forecasting of economic movements. Let us turn to a general discussion of the character of government investment under a compensatory spending program.

First of all, the meaning of the term "government investment": public investment signifies expenditure for enduring improvements, that is, any physical structure designed to yield utilities beyond one year [26]—the customary fiscal accounting period. Another name for the same type of expenditure is "capital expenditures."

Both terms are used in counterdistinction to "current expenditures." All durable improvements irrespective of monetary return are regarded as public investments. The factor of income yield becomes relevant only in a classification of governmental accounts into two distinct classes—the self-financing "capital account" as opposed to nonsupporting "capital account." Even here the existence or absence of a return on public capital outlays is frequently held to be irrelevant to their inclusion in the capital account.

Government capital investment clearly covers a very wide area. Within its scope are included everything from the development of public playgrounds to the construction of bridges, roads, drainage systems, battleships, and harbor improvements. Outlays for direct relief are generally considered to be current expenditures while expenditures on roads built by relief workers, even though there may exist an element of outright relief, are commonly placed under the investment category. Frequently the distinction between current and capital outlays loses its sharpness. Refinements are sometimes possible, and projects may be broken down into two categories—capital expenditure and noncapital, as were, for example, the outlays of the Works Progress Administration and other agencies in the 1940 federal budget which regarded (somewhat arbitrarily) three-fifths of these expenditures as asset-creating. It is virtually impossible to calculate the real incremental value to our national capital assets produced by a given expenditure. How much is a hospital worth, an irrigation project, or a new high school? The only practical accounting basis here is money cost.

In the decisions as to the composition of an investment and spend-

[26] A broader definition of capital expenditures appears in the writings of Pigou, Irving Fisher, and Marshall. Expenditures made for relief, and so forth, are regarded as capital outlays, since such payments are viewed as investments made to support "human" capital.

ing program, however, some sort of yardstick of relative social utility will have to be followed, however rough it may be. This is a somewhat elusive problem. The original determination, however, of the proper sphere of public investment and spending presents an even more complex problem. We can only briefly suggest two of the major criteria involved in this latter connection: (1) the minimization of possible adverse repercussions on private investment decisions, and (2) the relative urgency for government provision of various types of facilities. In a country like the United States, where the range of publicly undertaken services is highly circumscribed, it may very likely become necessary, under a large-scale compensatory spending program, to expand beyond the existing fields and enter into competition with private enterprise. The tendency, in discussing compensatory spending policy, to fail to go beyond the inaugural period of such a program has been particularly unfortunate. The implications of an expanding level of public outlays, which is bound to involve heightened competition with private enterprise, are of the utmost importance. This problem will be examined in Chapter V, along with other issues raised above.

In the government spending program earlier described (pump-priming) the financing of the program involved no very serious departure from budgetary orthodoxy. While an annual budgetary balance was to be sacrificed, the consequent depression debt was to be liquidated with the surpluses realized during the prosperous phase of the cycle. An annual budgetary balance was to be replaced with a cyclically balanced account—a fiscal program much more consonant with economic reality. The theoretical defense of this position was persuasive. There was but one source of difficulty—the possibility of the failure of the maturation of a recovery of sufficient proportions and duration to produce the required surpluses. The present theory is not posited on the basis of such a cyclical budgetary balance, but accepts the necessity of a continual rise in the outstanding public debt.[27] This belief marks a sharp break with conventional economic thought. The growth of public debt is held by advocates of compensatory spending, among other things, to be a measure of the increase in public assets.

[27] Hansen looks upon a rising level of national debt as a desirable goal in itself, since it provides an opportunity for favorable investment outlets. *Fiscal Policy and Business Cycles*, p. 160. Hansen contends that the English public debt in the nineteenth century was on balance an advantageous element. *Ibid.*, pp. 153-156.

THE CAPITAL-CURRENT BUDGET

The notion of a budgetary balance is incompatible with a secular investment and spending program of the type described. In line with this view it is necessary to segregate public outlays which are asset-creating from ordinary current or recurring expenditures. The adoption of a "capital-current" budget would give expression to this distinction. The capital side of the ledger would measure the changing asset picture of government, while the current ledger would accurately reflect operations on current account. Borrowing would presumably occur only for financing capital expenditures, while current operations would be met wholly through current revenues. Under a capital budget provision would be made for meeting interest charges and operating expenses out of current revenue. The flexibility required by a compensatory investment program would, it is asserted, be achieved through such a separation of accounts.[28]

Capital-current budgets have had a rather long history—the beginnings of the Scandinavian experience with this type of budget preceding the first World War. Such budgets have been adopted by numerous state and local governments in the United States. Various objections to this budgetary plan have been raised by public finance experts. We shall refer briefly to a few most widely entertained; (1) the double budgetary system is held to violate one of the fundamental considerations of budgetary theory—the need for budgetary unity which holds that a complete statement of all income and outlay must be summed up in *one* balance. This principle is based upon the fear of manipulation of the true budgetary position possible in a dual or multi-account budget. Balance is the paramount desideratum in such a system of accounts. This represents a basic and irreconcilable difference from the capital current budget and reflects a fundamental conflict of economic philosophy which cannot be resolved by discussions of budgetary principles. Under the one system a deficit is symptomatic of an unhealthy situation; under the other it is essential to economic well-being. The principle of "unity" is denied by advocates of compensatory spending. To them it is applicable only to an economy providing ample avenues to private investment, not one suffering from secular-stagnation.

---

[28] See Erik Lindahl's excellent presentation of the capital-current budget in his *Studies in the Theory of Money and Capital*, appendix on "*The Problem of Balancing the Budget.*"

SECULAR-STAGNATION

Another objection, previously referred to, concerns the validity of the use of the term "public asset." Since the distinction between capital and current expenditures rests upon the analogy with private business accounting,[29] it is considered necessary to separate government investment into two classes: (1) the category of capital outlay yielding a monetary return (or productive investment) as opposed to (2) the nonprofitable (or nonproductive) category. The latter class, it is held, is not properly classifiable as an "asset"—a term reserved for self-liquidating public investments alone. In the broad sense of the term *any* capital outlay which adds to the provision of community services is an asset, although in the strict accounting sense it is an "unproductive-asset" and should be excluded from the capital budget unless it is genuinely self-liquidating. This interpretation is held entirely arbitrary by the capital-budget adherents, in view of the fact that charges *could* be levied for a much wider range of public services than are now scheduled. For instance, it would be perfectly possible to place charges on the use of public parks, schools, conservation, and so forth, and to derive sufficient revenue to make the projects self-supporting (although it would surely serve to limit the number of such projects). The assessment of charges for a very wide range of public services, however, is held contrary to public policy, since one of the chief factors behind the creation of free public services is precisely the inability of the pricing mechanism to allocate successfully certain utilities in a socially desirable manner. Most public services increase the productive resources of the community and are more or less directly related to the private economy. Public capital expenditures, according to the perspective of the secular-stagnation school, may be looked upon as overhead costs in the operation of a capitalist economy.

Strict adherence to the distinction between productive and nonproductive investments can best be observed when the government is engaged in a wide variety of business activities to which there are attached regular costs. Swedish accounting practice, for example, has differentiated between self-liquidating and non-self-liquidating investment activities, treating the latter as current expenditures to be financed out of current income, although here freedom of action has, in consequence, been rather seriously limited. Myrdal and other critics of this "conservative" system favor adoption of the Danish

[29] See Hansen's discussion of Professor Pedersen's article in the *Weltwirtschaftliches Archiv*, May, 1937, *Fiscal Policy and Business Cycles*, pp. 140–142.

procedure,[20] which does not differentiate between productive and nonproductive outlays.

Acceptance of the orientation of the capital-budget advocates is rewarded by partial liberation from the chains of fiscal orthodoxy. How valid, however, is their position? Have the proponents of modern budgetary procedure delivered us from the morass of outdated shibboleths, or have they merely fallen victims to an attractive illusion? In reading these pages Professor J. M. Clark has been prompted to remark upon "the peculiar magic whereby *fiscal* debt is sanctified by being correlated with *nonfiscal* 'assets.' " Is the above procedure any more than "fiscal self-deception, like the old English sinking fund, which was maintained when they had to borrow to maintain it?" Furthermore, Professor Clark questions whether the general considerations of social productivity described above justify counting an asset as productive for fiscal purposes except by some such test: "Do they cause existing tax rates to yield more revenue?" or "Do they furnish taxable income that doesn't involve raising tax rates on existing income?"

The foregoing formulation suggests that advocates of deficit-financing feel the need of a sanctifying ritual to support it. It is, of course, perfectly correct that the most important reason underlying advocacy of the double-budget scheme is the recognition of the necessity of reducing popular concern over the increasing volume of peacetime public debt. The accounting ritual observed tends to obfuscate the issue. It is important to get behind the forms assumed by the capital-current budget and examine the essence of the proposal. The issues raised above involve considerations more fundamental than can conveniently be related to budgetary principles at this point in the discussion. No resolution will be attempted until we reach Chapter V, which is concerned with the broader issues involved in financing a compensatory fiscal program.

Will the level of debt increase interminably, will continuing deficits (for capital investment) be realized year in and year out? No, not necessarily. Fluctuations in economic activity will certainly continue, although, according to advocates of the Hansenian viewpoint, less violently than during previous decades. While a balanced or overbalanced budget may possibly be realized in very favorable years, the compensatory theory does not require this development, and it is

[20] See Brinley Thomas's discussion in his volume *Monetary Policy and Crises*, London, 1936.

irrelevant to the success of such a program. The prospect of continuing deficits will depend upon the relative magnitude of public investment as compared to private investment. We may conceive of various stages of compensatory policy in which the proportion of public investment to private investment is small, moderate, or large over a number of years; the possibility that an expansion in the private economy will effect a complete cessation of public investment will obviously depend upon the relative sphere occupied by the latter. Only in the event of a reversal of the present direction of the so-called factors of economic progress will it be possible to retire from a compensatory program. Temporary withdrawal from such a program, however, may be desirable, if possible, in the event of a brief resurgence in private investment.

Moderate fluctuations in private investment need not be accompanied by corresponding adjustment in the volume of public investment unless the economy is functioning at a level very close to full employment. If the compensatory scheme is designed to produce a condition of relative prosperity (and this would seem the wisest course for the supporters of the above program to pursue), the private economy could expand to some extent. In the event that private outlays were introduced gradually there would be small danger of inducing any serious price inflation.[31] While the orientation of the compensatory scheme is for the most part on the secular level, some response would presumably have to be forthcoming in the event of more than moderate cyclical fluctuations. Public investment would have to be adjusted to marked cyclical movements. However, it could be argued that the very existence of a substantial volume of continuing public investment representing a substantial portion of total net capital formation, should serve as a stabilizing factor. With the provision of a relatively stable base of government capital investment, insensitive for the most part to cyclical swings, the amplitude of economic fluctuations should be reduced. This development, however, will clearly not render the economy immune to dislocations deriving from possible breakdowns in certain industries or vertical maladjustments and such factors as wars, and so forth.

The susceptibility of a compensatory program to cyclical manipula-

[31] The specter of inflation (meaning here an appreciable price rise) is not present in the same manner that threatens in the case of wartime or defense spending. In the latter case time is infinitely more pressing and speed in operations, of the essence. In peacetime spending the time factor is subject to control. Minor bottlenecks can be solved in time.

tion is relatively limited. But the factor of timing does not assume the same strategic significance as is attached to it in the public works stabilization or pump-priming programs. The greater the relative sphere of the total economy within governmental scope, the less severe are likely to be economic fluctuations. In the initial period of a compensatory investment program of comparatively meager proportions, cyclical fluctuations are not likely to be much reduced. If the program, in its early stages, be mistakenly directed primarily to the pursuance of cyclical stabilization objectives, it is possible that economic fluctuations may be accelerated rather than damped by poor timing. However, it is hardly likely that there would exist any desire to stabilize activity at a level far below full employment.

We have greatly simplified the problem under consideration by neglecting such fundamental factors as business psychology, the factor of risk, public response to increasing debt, and so forth. These will be taken up in a later section. No attempt has been made above to evaluate the fiscal doctrines of the stagnation school. We have attempted to systematize and round out, in some respects, the views of the group.

IV. A CRITIQUE OF THE SECULAR-STAGNATION DOCTRINE

THE PRESENT CHAPTER is devoted to an analysis of the more controversial aspects of the secular-stagnation theory. How valid, we may inquire, is the position presented by Professor Hansen and his school? How reliable is the evidence submitted? Such inquiry properly precedes an analysis of the extent to which fiscal policy provides a solution to the problem of secular stagnation. This latter question will be considered in Chapter VII.

Let us examine the three conditions upon which the stagnation doctrine rests before turning to an analysis of the curative properties of compensatory public spending. We shall examine in order: (1) the role of technological progress, (2) the significance of the altered rate of population growth, and (3) the import of the closing of the frontier and foreign outlets for capital investment upon the level of business activity and the prospects for our economic institutions.

ECONOMIC PROGRESS AND TECHNOLOGICAL SATURATION

Hansen's analysis of the factors of economic progress proceeds very largely in technological terms. The saturation point for an industry is apparently dictated by technical factors and recognized growth curves quite independently of the specific institutional economic framework. These exogenous considerations are presumed to operate with relative autonomy affected only in minor degree by changing cost and price situations, the profits outlook, the political setting, and a host of other considerations. We are thus enslaved in the mesh of uncontrollable and unpredictable factors of economic progress.

Noting the earlier impetus realized from rapid population growth and foreign investment, Professor Hansen states that

> The outlets of new investment are rapidly narrowing down to those created by the progress of technology. . . . When giant new industries have spent their force, it *may* take a long time before something else of equal magnitude emerges. In fact nothing has emerged in the decade in which we are now living.[1]

[1] "Progress and Declining Population," *American Economic Review*, XXIX (March, 1939), 9–11.

In describing the role of technological progress Hansen frequently fails to distinguish between the investment impact of new industries and products and that of improvements in existing methods of production. The second category is surprisingly enough not infrequently overlooked, and economic progress is assumed to comprehend merely new inventions and industries. There is, of course, no reason to believe that for recent years the aggregate new investment attributable to this area is smaller than that for the former type of economic progress.

Industrial and technological saturation, as propounded by Hansen, appears to be divorced from institutional concomitants—resulting, instead, solely from various exogenous factors. Price phenomena, cost-price relationships, wage policies, and so forth are deemed to be of only nominal importance in their effect upon the course of industrial development. The level of investment and economic activity is dependent—almost completely—upon the pace of technological change.[2]

Hansen specifically denies the importance of cyclical changes in cost-price relations in the heavy goods industries as related to other prices as an explanation for the downturn. He argues that the reduction of sticky prices and wages will not aid recovery, but on the other hand "may intensify the cyclical problem because of the effect of such price changes upon business expectations."[3] This position flows naturally from Professor Hansen's contention that cyclical maladjustments in price-cost relationships are the *consequences* rather than the *causes* of the downturn. The basic explanation here, again, is to be found rather in the external factors surrounding the conditions of economic progress.

Hansen, however, while not conceding the importance of cyclical price adjustments, holds that structural price flexibility is essential if the full gains of economic progress are to be realized.[4] This latter type of flexibility involves the secular adjustment of prices to changes in the cost of production.

In contending that rigid prices should be maintained and falling prices be raised, Hansen avoids the entire issue of the contributory responsibility of price relationships in setting off the decline. It is

---

[2] "Investment expenditures . . . are determined by outside factors having to do with changes in the real factors inherent in economic progress . . ." Hansen, *Fiscal Policy and Business Cycles*, p. 329.

[3] *Ibid.*, p. 324.   [4] *Ibid.*, p. 314.

CRITIQUE OF SECULAR-STAGNATION

just this function, however, which needs to be determined. As will be suggested in the discussion of several turning points in the period between 1933 and 1940, price disparities exercised a powerful force in shaping the business cycle. Hansen, himself, elsewhere [5] attributes primary importance to price developments in shaping the 1937 recession. The case for maintaining the price relationships prevalent at the end of the cyclical upswing would be persuasive only in the event that a satisfactory balance could be demonstrated at that time.

Hansen departs from his advocacy of price maintenance to the extent of acknowledging that an orderly program of cost-price adjustment combined with monetary and fiscal policy designed to maintain the level of economic activity does facilitate recovery.[6] This amendment, however, appears somewhat at odds with his insistence that price levels be maintained. It would seem that Professor Hansen is here thinking in terms of what he designates as structural price relationships. Unfortunately, no clear line of demarcation can be established between secular and cyclical price flexibility. No suggestion is offered in explanation of the frequency with which structural price changes should occur or how such changes can be distinguished from cyclical adaptations.

In describing the consequences of "arbitrary" price reductions Hansen stresses the elimination of marginal firms.[7] No definition, however, of "arbitrary" price cuts is submitted, and no systematic analysis of the resulting disinvestment process as opposed to the offsetting favorable repercussions is attempted. Is the maintenance of marginal firms at the cost of excessive administered price levels a wise policy? Professor Hansen denies that a reduction in consumers' goods prices can increase employment—this goal can only be the end product of technological advance. Not only does this contention ignore the prospective gains available under elastic demand schedules but it also dismisses the price reductions (under competitive conditions) incidental to the economies of increased scale of production.

The Keynesian reduction in the marginal efficiency of capital (concomitant upon the accumulation of great stocks of capital) is viewed by Hansen as approaching zero in the absence of economic progress. But it can be shown that there was no lack of vigor in the pace of technological progress throughout the decade of the thirties. The number and variety of innovations during that decade compared favorably

[5] *Full Recovery or Stagnation?* chap. xvi. [6] *Ibid.*, p. 322. [7] *Ibid.*, p. 333.

with any comparable preceding period. There is no need to relate in detail the huge number of inventions, improved processes, innovations, and so forth, for the period.[8] One is prompted to observe that only a small portion of the total potential new investment demand implicit in these innovations found actual expression. The absence of a hospitable investment climate may be offered as explanation for this unrealized development. Certainly, it would appear difficult to establish any great fall in the marginal efficiency of capital as related to the materialization of technological advance.

To the extent that the WPA study of recent technological change is correct in its contention that contemporary technical advance is predominantly *capital-saving* as contrasted with the more characteristic *labor-saving* type of earlier technological change, the marginal efficiency of capital is *raised* rather than reduced, as asserted. Although, paradoxically, the aggregate demand for capital may, in consequence, be reduced. Such reduction in the demand for capital as transpires may be attributed, however, to market imperfections rather than to any saturation of opportunity for new capital investment per se. It is only in a static sense involving a comparison of the capital funds required to effect a *given* increase in output, assuming an unaltered technology on the one hand and a capital-saving innovation on the other, that a decline in demand for capital can be assumed.

Professor Hansen, while tending to minimize the role of price maladjustments in cyclical and longer-run economic behavior (quite surprisingly) notes considerable impairment in the functioning of the price system since the first World War.[9] No clarification, unfortunately, is offered as to the contributory importance of this alleged development for long-run stagnation. If it were true that competitive elements in our economy have declined in recent decades,[10] the explanation of the stagnation of the 1930's would be greatly facilitated. It is impossible, however, to produce statistical evidence of increasing price rigidity in recent decades.[11] Investigation of the prevalence of

[8] See United States, Work Projects Administration, *Industrial Change and Employment Opportunity—a Selected Bibliography*, Sec. II.
[9] *Fiscal Policy and Business Cycles*, p. 46.
[10] As contended in A. R. Burns, *The Decline of Competition;* Gardiner C. Means, "Price Inflexibility and the Requirements of a Stabilizing Monetary Policy," *Journal American Statistical Association*, XXX (June, 1935), 401–413; Ezekiel, *Jobs for All;* and Simons, *A Positive Program for Laissez-Faire.*
[11] Rigidities, inflexibilities, administered prices we have always had with us, along with prices determined in greater or lesser degree by the play of competition among buyers and sellers. The area of competition has doubtless expanded and contracted, but it is

CRITIQUE OF SECULAR-STAGNATION 49

price inflexibility have failed to disclose any growth in the extent of price stability.[12] Flexible prices have characterized certain groups of products, primarily agricultural and other raw materials, while administered or noncompetitively determined prices have been located primarily in semifinished or finished goods industries.[13]

Without assuming any increase in price inflexibility (although this development is not necessarily precluded by the foregoing statistical studies), we may inquire as to the incidence of imperfect competition. Nominally, the chief pressure of administered prices is exerted by way of interference with the market's tendency—under competitive conditions—to gravitate to the equilibrium point, once that equilibrium has been disturbed.[14] Thus, while inflexible prices may have had no direct role in immediately precipitating the downturn, their existence tends to prolong and intensify the recession or depression. In the event that cost-price maladjustments have helped bring on a business decline, failure to rectify such distortions clearly acts to extend the recession's duration.

Administered prices, moreover, tend to reduce the level of economic activity at every point in the cycle, although the curtailment of output effected escapes attention during relatively prosperous periods. The maintenance of prices, at the expense of a decline in demand for products enjoying an elastic demand schedule, involves an inevitable intensification in the pace of the recession. In the absence of price adjustments, an upturn must await a revival from the demand side prompted by obsolescence and depreciation requirements or else the materialization of new developments affecting the profits outlook.

While it is difficult to demonstrate a clear-cut growth in the relative scope of administered prices in recent decades, the same is not true of

probable that truly competitive prices never formed more than a small minority of the prices at which good and services have actually changed hands, through the ages. And that includes the era of industrial and commercial expansion of the nineteenth and twentieth centuries." F. C. Mills, "Relation of Size of Plants to Prices—Discussion," *American Economic Review*, XXVI (Supplement, March, 1936), 62–64.

[12] Humphrey, "The Nature and Meaning of Rigid Prices, 1890–1933," *Journal of Political Economy*, XLV (October, 1937), 651–661; Mason, "Price Inflexibility," *Review of Economic Statistics*, XX (May, 1938), 53–64; and Tucker, "The Essential Historical Facts about 'Sensitive' and 'Administered' Prices," *Annalist*, LI (February 4, 1938), 195–196.

[13] The frequency of price changes, however, is not the sole criteria of price flexibility. The relative importance of certain classes of prices and price changes will vary over a period of years. See Ralph C. Wood, "Tuckers 'Reasons' of Price Rigidity," *American Economic Review*, XXVIII (December, 1938), 663–673.

[14] See Ezekiel, "The Cobweb Theorem," *Quarterly Journal of Economics*, LII (February, 1938), 278–279.

the labor market. For, paralleling the rise of the CIO, there has occurred since 1935 a remarkable increase of institutional controls over wage rates. Organized labor has countered industry's system of price control with a huge and relatively successful drive of its own. Such legislation, too, as the Wages and Hours Act and the Unemployment Insurance Act plus the unprecedented WPA and PWA emergency programs have all tended to reduce some of the former wage flexibility. But perhaps more important (in terms of the impact on economic activity) than the growth of administered wage rates has been the response of business to labor's new power. For in the years of the Roosevelt administration the preferred position of employers has suffered a setback (loaded with manifold implications for the future) at the hands of labor. Professor Slichter, in commenting on this phenomenon, states: [16]

In the first place, the very fact that a great shift in power was going on created uncertainty concerning the long-term yield on capital and hence created an abnormal preference for short-term production plans. In this way, uncertainty narrowed investment and reduced temporarily the marginal return on capital. . . . In the second place, the shift in economic power altered in many plants the control of managements over labor costs and increased the difficulty of converting a rise of output into profits. . . . When profits come hard, the disposition to venture is weak. . . . The lesser success of enterprises in converting a rise of business into profits after 1933 than after 1921 is explained by a variety of circumstances, but very largely by the movements of labor efficiency and wages. Physical productivity per man hour grew twice as fast after 1921 as after 1933 or 1934, but wage rates went up twice as rapidly in the second period as in the first. The differences were not entirely compensated by price movements.

Of comparable importance to labor's assumption of new power has been the impact of increased tax burdens on business enterprise. These two developments, secular in character, represent perhaps the most outstanding changes in our economic environment although denied a major place in Hansen's analysis. The tax changes of the last two decades have exerted a significant influence upon business investment decisions. Professor Angell states:

There is . . . no major line of escape from the conclusion . . . that in all important cases, actual or even merely expected increases in those taxes of which the burden varies even roughly with individual or busi-

[16] "The Conditions of Expansion," *American Economic Review*, XXXII (Supplement, March, 1942), 4-5.

ness income from assets must necessarily reduce the volume of subsequent new private investment below what it would otherwise have been.[16]

Risk capital was especially discouraged by a federal corporate tax structure which neglected adequate loss allowance and averaging of income over a sufficiently long period of years for tax purposes.

The tax measures of the New Deal have tended to be more concerned with redistribution of income and other social objectives than with business incentives. The emphasis has been upon the propensity to consume rather than on the marginal efficiency of capital. Despite the stated objective of achieving a more progressive federal tax structure, however, the opposite has transpired. The proceeds of direct taxation declined relative to the yield of indirect taxes during the thirties.[17] For while the higher rates applied to corporate and private income were reflected in greater tax receipts, new and increased commodity and Social Security taxes increased the relative importance of indirect taxation.[18] The chief explanation for the greater burden placed on corporate and personal incomes was to be found in the heightened revenue demands necessitated by expanded depression outlays.

Increasing and heavy federal corporate tax levies are no recent phenomena, but trace back to the first World War. Prior to that time corporation tax rates were virtually painless. In the years 1909–1916 the effective federal corporate tax rates averaged about 1 percent. The war years 1917–1921 witnessed a sharp jump to an average effective rate of 23.5 percent. Corporate tax rates fell in the following years, but were maintained well above the prewar level, averaging some 11.6 percent (effective rate) in the years 1922–1932. Contrary to many assertions the corporate tax rate did not rise sharply during the Roosevelt administration. The average effective corporation income tax rate rose only moderately, to 15.3 percent, for the period 1933–1937.[19] A rise from 14.2 percent to 17.3 percent took place between 1933 and 1937. A further increase was realized during 1938 and 1939. While

[16] *Investment and Business Cycles*, p. 278

[17] See United States, Treasury, *Annual Report of Secretary of the Treasury*, 1942, and United States, Temporary National Economic Committee, Monograph No. 9, *Taxation of Corporate Enterprise*, by Clifford J. Hynning, Table 1, p. 8.

[18] During the late nineteen twenties about 60 percent of all federal revenue was derived from direct taxation, while the share fell to about 30-odd percent in 1934 and 1935 and to some 45 percent in 1937 and 1938.

[19] The above statistics are derived from *ibid.*, Table II, p. 11.

the study referred to does not show the effective rates for the above years, a rise to roughly 18 percent is probable. Statutory rates ranged from 16.5 to 19 percent in 1938 and 1939.

The total tax burden upon the economy, federal as well as state and local taxation, has long been rising and in the last two decades has assumed significant proportions. Table 1 traces this development.

TABLE 1

PERCENTAGE OF TAX COLLECTIONS TO NATIONAL INCOME [a]

Year	Federal	State and Local	Total
1910	1.9	4.5	6.4
1913	1.9	4.6	6.5
1922	5.8	6.5	12.3
1928	4.1	7.5	11.6
1930	5.1	9.6	14.7
1934	5.7	11.4	17.1
1938	9.1	13.5	22.7

[a] After table prepared by Simon Kuznets in "National Income and Taxable Capacity," *American Economic Review*, XXXII (Supplement, March, 1942), 37–75.

Mr. Kuznets notes the discouragement to enterprise stemming from a general increase in the tax burden.

An increase in direct or indirect taxation means a deprivation of individuals and enterprises of a greater power to save or spend, and the desire for such power has been a powerful motive in the operation of the economic system. It is also possible to argue that a growing progressivity of the tax system, affecting particularly the categories of savers and investors and increasing the uncertain risks, serves as a curb upon capital formation and hence upon the growth in the productive power of the nation.[20]

Mr. Kuznets predicts a substantial increase in the future ratio of all taxes collected to the current flow of income payments over the ratios of the nineteen twenties and nineteen thirties.

The long-term increase in tax levies as a portion of the national dividend is a phenomenon by no means restricted to the United States; it has been evident in practically every country for which statistics are available.[21] This development has been prompted by expanded public outlays for a greater variety of government services, enlarged welfare expenditures, relief and recovery appropriations, and mili-

[20] Kuznets, "National Income and Taxable Capacity," *American Economic Review*, XXX (Supplement, March, 1942), 59.
[21] See League of Nations, *World Economic Survey 1938–1939*, chap. ii.

tary outlays. In the postwar period this trend is likely to continue. Thus, it seems certain that tax collections will continue to be a major factor affecting business decisions.

Of special significance in accounting for the stagnation of the thirties were the psychological hazards and the so-called political impediments which prevailed during most of the decade. One of the outstanding characteristics of the thirties was the pessimism which dominated the period. The heritage of the collapse of the early thirties colored the entire decade with a thick dark gloom which never wholly lifted, even during the latter years, despite the rise in business activity. After the initial period of stunned distress, business slowly collected its wits, but failed to retrieve its earlier spirit. The optimism of the twenties was succeeded by an intense pessimism mirroring the popular reappraisal of the prospects of business enterprise. The termination of the growing myth of unending new-era prosperity which arose during the twenties, gave rise to a cautious, conservative brand of business policy contrasting sharply with the aggressive, anticipatory, expansive operations of the twenties. Business policy during the thirties was timid and cautious, rigidly geared to current demand, and unresponsive to speculative ventures. Such a psychological reaction is eminently understandable, but it should be appreciated that although a product of the depression, the pessimism of this period constituted a positive factor aggravating the economic outlook. Nurtured in an environment of blatant optimism, the psychological equilibrium of business was rudely upset, and a revulsion of sentiment to the other extreme set in. The manic-depressive tendency of business was never more apparent than in the decades of the twenties and the thirties.

A further psychological hazard to business confidence was the apparent inability of the business community to reconcile or to adapt itself readily to the swift pace of change in the scope and character of the relation of the federal government to the economy. Objection was voiced to numerous measures introduced by the Roosevelt administration. The chief subjects of business criticism were: (*a*) New Deal labor legislation (NLRA, Wages and Hours Act; Social Security Act) and the prolabor attitude exhibited; (*b*) the government's spending program and consequent deficits; (*c*) new tax measures; (*d*) security exchange regulations;[22] and (*e*) the generally unfavorable attitude toward big business frequently manifested by the administration (al-

[22] Especially allegations of SEC burdens on small promotions.

though in time it was appreciated in more sophisticated quarters that the New Deal's bark was more prominent than its bite).

Unfortunately the accumulated backlog of social legislation and reform had piled so high in this country that the opening of the floodgates after such a long arid period inevitably started a tide which proved difficult for the business community to deal with. It was not generally appreciated that it was primarily our backwardness which caused this concentration of legislation rather than a hostile or left-wing government. We were merely catching up with the reforms realized long before by older capitalist nations. However, be this as it may, the administration stirred apprehension in the minds of many businessmen over the future course of governmental intervention. Frequently, too, the motives of the administration were obscured and unreasonable fears aroused. Unwarranted and inexcusably bitter struggles ensued between the administration and various business interests over a wide variety of economic and social objectives.

The important requisite of stability and harmony in the relations between business and government to which business had been accustomed for several Republican administrations was conspicuously absent. The limited vision of particular business groups served to nourish the flames of controversy. While uncertainty and insecurity were inevitable during a period of such rapid change, a more flexible response by business would have served to reduce the impact of these disrupting elements; instead, various business leaders, by their stubborn resistance to change, contributed to an aggravation of the task of adjusting to an altered environment.

The constantly increasing international tension throughout the thirties, terminating in the outbreak of war, acted as a major deterrent to new investment and economic activity in general. While the mounting international uncertainty prompted huge military expenditures stimulating business activity, the constant threat that a major conflict might emerge from any one of the numerous *minor* wars and hostile episodes of the decade served to instill an atmosphere of pervasive apprehension. Business in this country certainly manifested no illusion over wartime profits nor did it entertain any belief in the desirability of war-stimulated prosperity. It was interesting to observe the restrained enthusiasm, even pessimism, of American businessmen in the face of prosperity levels in 1940 and 1941.

We are obliged to reject Professor Hansen's explanation of the

CRITIQUE OF SECULAR-STAGNATION

stagnation of the thirties as due to the saturation of investment opportunities. While there can be no question with respect to the central importance of the great technological developments such as the railroads and automobile and electric utilities industries in shaping the pattern of economic life in the past, the failure of the appearance of equally potent industries in the last decade (if this proves to be true) does not necessarily signify stagnation or an end to economic progress. No evidence has been submitted to indicate that the pace of technological progress has slowed down or that great unexploited opportunities for new capital investment were not available throughout the nineteen thirties.

It is highly unlikely, however, that we will again see the materialization of a single invention or industry capable of absorbing as great a *share* of our total resources as did, for example, the railroad development. While in absolute terms the enormous capital investment which found its way into the railroads may be equaled in the future in some other field, our total capital resources have so expanded as to prevent such a development from exercising the same dominating influence as was true at an earlier period. In this sense we may be said to have entered into a more mature stage of economic development. Prosperity can no longer be achieved by expansion in one or two major industries, but must be the product of a widely diversified expansion.

Insofar as our capital stock has been greatly enlarged in the last several decades, it may be argued that imperfect competition and trade restraints weigh correspondingly more heavily upon the economy. This may be attributed to the declining impetus of an expansion limited to any one sector of the economy—"declining" in a purely quantitative sense. Thus, it may be argued that administered price policies and trade restraints exercise an increasing secular influence.

The outlook for technological innovation has perhaps never been more promising than it is at present. The horizon is brimming over with a virtually inexhaustible variety of new inventions, innovations, new products, and improved processes apparently destined not only to create a demand for vast new capital investment but to recreate our world as well. The postwar world appears likely to be engulfed in a surge of technological change such as we have never seen. Partially attributable to the scientific acceleration resulting from the war, partly, on the other hand, to the necessary sidetracking of innovations to conserve strategic resources, and finally to the failure to exploit fully the technical advances during the depression-ridden decade of the thirties, there has been accumulated a stock of scientific discoveries guaranteed to astonish all but those actively interested in this field.

Among the most promising advances may be listed the following: [23] (1) synthetic raw materials derived from basic organic materials, such as synthetic rubber, nylon, and plastics; (2) commercial aviation and the family "flivver" plane; (3) radiotelephony including the "walkie-talkie" and television sets; (4) prefabricated housing; and (5) synthetic foods and vitamins.

In expressing pessimism over the prospects of adequate investment outlets in a high-savings economy such as ours, Hansen notes the great growth in recent decades of the importance of institutionalized savings and internal corporate financing. New security flotations and banking loans to enterprise have correspondingly declined. The uneven flow of savings to various sectors of the economy as well as the concentration of investment decisions in a relatively small number of hands has operated to restrict competition and reduce the aggregate volume of new investment.[24] This development is partly the consequence of legal limitations placed upon the disposition of funds of insurance companies and other financial institutions as well as the conservative investment policies characteristic of such organizations. With this analysis the author is in complete agreement. The remedy, at least in part, may perhaps be found in such proposals as that made by A. A. Berle, Jr., for the creation of a system of "capital credit banks" extending government credit to private and corporate borrowers willing to undertake new investment.[25]

POPULATION GROWTH AND NEW INVESTMENT

Another basic explanation for the stagnation of the thirties, according to Professor Hansen, is to be found in the reduced rate of population growth.[26] The rate of population increase for the United States in the last decade experienced a substantial decline; the rise in the total population in the decade of the thirties being only 7 percent as

[23] See *Fortune*, Vol. XXVI, No. 6 (Supplement for December, 1942), The United States in a New World, appendix on Technology and Post-war Life.

[24] See United States, Temporary National Economic Committee, Monograph No. 37, *Saving, Investment, and National Income*, by Oscar L. Altman, Part III.

[25] See "A Banking System for Capital and Capital Credit," United States, Temporary National Economic Committee, Hearings, Part 9, Exhibit No. 620, pp. 4067, 4068, 4072 and 4078.

[26] Hansen, "Progress and Declining Population," *American Economic Review*, XXIX (March, 1939), 1–15.

compared with 16 percent for the previous decade and appreciably greater growth rates for earlier decades. Economic opinion has progressed to the polar opposite of the early Malthusian enunciation as to the imminent danger of the pressure of population upon the means of subsistence. It is contended by Professor Hansen and others of his school that the above sharp fall in the rate of population expansion has resulted in a decline in the demand for new net capital investment from the level which would have obtained with a continuation of the earlier rate of growth. The argument is a simple one. "A rapidly growing population will demand a much larger per capita volume of new residential building construction than will a stationary population." [27] This principle applies to other types of new capital investment. This extensive demand for new capital investment is credited with a good share of responsibility for past economic expansion. Hansen estimates that the population growth in the second half of the nineteenth century in the United States was responsible for about 60 percent of the total volume of capital formation. With respect to Europe the figure is somewhat less—about 40 percent.[28]

Accepting the above estimates for purposes of convenience, it is seen that impact of population increase on economic expansion is of tremendous importance.[29] Granted the stated contribution of the growth of extensive demand in the past, does that necessarily establish a similar current relationship? Professor Hansen implies that had population grown in the past decade of the thirties at a pace equivalent to that of the previous decade, general economic conditions during the years 1930–1940 would have been substantially better. How correct is this point of view? [30]

All other things equal, the greater the population, the greater the potential total volume of economic activity. A correlated maxim is that the demand for new capital investment is in part a function of the rate of increase in population growth. A rapidly expanding population has obviously greater *requirements* than those for a stable or moderately expanding population. To meet the needs of increasing

[27] *Ibid.*, p. 7.   [28] *Ibid.*, p. 8.

[29] "In the beginning stages of modern capitalism both the deepening and the widening processes of capital formation were developing side by side. But in its later stages the deepening process, taking the economy as a whole, rapidly diminished. And now with the rapid cessation of population growth even the widening process may slow down. Moreover it is possible that capital-saving inventions may cause capital formation in many industries to lag behind the increase in output." *Ibid.*, p. 7.

[30] See Sweezy, "Population Growth and Investment Opportunity," *Quarterly Journal of Economics*, LV (November, 1940), 64–79, for critique of the above population analysis.

numbers, new capital investment will ordinarily have to be undertaken and existing plant facilities more fully utilized than would have otherwise been the case. Through the operation of the acceleration principle new investment will thus be induced. In an economy apparently languishing because of a deficiency of new capital investment, the needs arising from extensive growth of consumer demand may produce a substantial improvement in economic behavior. While the economy may be overbuilt with respect to the requirements of the existing population, a rapidly expanding population may effectively remedy this situation. Entrepreneurs, furthermore, are keenly aware of movements of the total population and plan their production schedules in anticipation of such developments.

The above analysis (while somewhat simplified) is, on the surface, eminently persuasive. The economy in the past *was* buoyed up by rapid population growth. The recent decline in the pace of expansion has, it is asserted, brought in its wake an inevitable weakening of demand, not only for consumers' goods but for producers' goods as well. A rapid rate of population expansion guarantees, as it were, a corresponding new and assured rise in the demand for new capital investment.[81]

Various exceptions may be arrayed against the preceding argument. Of fundamental importance is the need for distinguishing between *potential* and *effective* demand.[32] There is no a priori ground for assuming an identity between the two. Only that consumer demand fortified by ready funds [33] affects the market; that portion of total potential demand which remains inarticulate exerts no effect upon the market. If there were any assurance that in the depression decade, 1930–1940, larger families would have guaranteed a higher volume of effective demand for durable consumers' goods, such as housing, refrigerators, automobiles, and so forth, the validity of the population argument would be strengthened. However, there is a strong presumption that larger families (higher birth rate) would not have produced any comparable increase in total consumer demand. The conse-

---

[81] It has been suggested that a rapidly aging population also requires a greater capital investment, since, for example, the children of a household later dwell in separate households of their own. The actual results under such circumstances will depend upon the rate at which dwelling space is made available through vacancies created by death, modified by qualitative housing demands.

[32] Hansen recognizes the force of this distinction in his latest volume, *Fiscal Policy and Business Cycles*, p. 248.

[33] Including borrowing ability.

CRITIQUE OF SECULAR-STAGNATION 59

quences of alterations in the birth rate must be examined in the light of varying propensities to consume for different income groups.

For the income groups where the propensity to consume is unity or thereabout (low-income groups), an enlargement in the size of the family by the birth of another child will not ordinarily increase the aggregate family expenditures. Rather, an increase in the size of the family would leave total family outlays unchanged and would effect instead a reduction in the per capita expenditures of the other members of the family. Total family expenditures can only be raised by an increase in the size of the family when the propensity to consume of a household is something less than unity. Only if a household be left with net savings at the end of a year is it possible that an increase in the size of the family may produce a greater annual volume of expenditures—with a consequent reduction in the aggregate amount of savings. No assurance, however, may be placed upon such a development, since the family may be following a definite savings program which may survive despite its increased size.

It is only among the relatively high-income groups, where savings accrue without sacrifice, that a growth in the size of the family makes an expansion of consumption outlay likely.

In the middle-income classes there is a choice between a reallocation of total family expenditures and increasing total family expenditures at the expense of a reduction in annual savings.

With regard to the general pattern of consumption for the American economy, we can say that roughly two-thirds of the entire population have had propensities to consume approximating one.[34] Larger families, for the most part, would produce a rearrangement of the existing pattern of expenditures without effecting a rise in overall consumer outlays. Only in the event of a rise in the birth rate in the upper third of the income brackets could we rightfully assume that the propensity to consume would be increased somewhat and savings correspondingly reduced. It follows, therefore, that the total volume of consumer outlays of about two-thirds of the population will be relatively uninfluenced by a rise in the birth rate.[35] Increased consumer

[34] See United States, National Resources Committee, *Consumer Expenditures in United States*. Sixty percent of the population in 1935–1936 had incomes of less than $1,275; 70 percent had incomes below $1,540. The former group operated at a deficit, while the group earning $1,275–$1,540 realized very slight savings.

[35] This conclusion is somewhat more rigorous than the facts probably warrant. It is not true that every member of a group which as a whole spends 100 percent of its income also spends his entire income at all times. Some individuals will be saving, others going

expenditures attributable to larger families will be derived wholly from the expansion of outlays by the wealthy one-third of the population.

There exists no necessary connection between the rate of population growth and the aggregate money demand for consumer goods. There is no fixed ratio between the rate of new residential construction and the rate of population growth. Larger families may result merely in greater crowding, lower per capita standards of living, and so forth. We need not review the conditions in which the characteristically large, low-wage, and relief families existed during the 1930's. If the average relief family was "blessed" with an additional offspring, the well-being of the other members of the household would consequently be reduced, aggregate expenditures remaining unaltered, unless the family's relief stipend was correspondingly increased.

A higher birth rate for the largest portion of the population would mean a greater demand for certain commodities and a consequent fall in demand for others. More milk, baby carriages, diaper pins, teething rings, and toys, among other things, would be required in a society enjoying a higher birth rate, while certain sacrifices would have to be made by way of financing the above, perhaps by reductions in tobacco purchases, automobiles, electric refrigerators, and the like.

The economic consequences of a rise in population from sources other than an increase in the birth rate, namely, by immigration, may now be briefly examined. The problem may be framed in this manner: If the rate of population growth experienced during the twenties had been maintained during the decade of the thirties, through a compensating rise in the volume of immigration, despite a decline in domestic fertility rates, would this development have shortened the duration of the depression? We shall assume, in line with the character of earlier immigration, that the newcomers to our shores are primarily job hunters rather than immediate sources of substantial per capita demand for durable and semiluxury goods. With their background of lower living standards, they are not likely to be purchasers of such types of commodities until they have been employed for some time and succumbed to the higher American standard of

---

into debt for the purchase of a home, while others will be dissaving funds accumulated for a "rainy day," and so forth. But, in general, the response to an additional mouth to feed will follow the pattern indicated above.

CRITIQUE OF SECULAR-STAGNATION

living.[36] If no employment is found, they constitute drags upon the incomes of their relatives or become public charges.

The receptiveness of an economy to immigrant labor, or, to put it differently, the capacity of a nation to absorb profitably new job seekers varies from period to period, not only with respect to cyclical fluctuation but with regard to secular economic changes as well. There is no need to dwell upon the obviously greater capacity of the economy to absorb entrants to the labor market during a period of business prosperity than during a period of depression or declining business activity. There is some question, however, as to whether the long-run capacity of the American economy to absorb labor has declined.

The calculation of the *optimum* size of the laboring force for a given economy, at a particular stage of the development of the arts, is at best a most complex problem. It is very difficult to determine at what point a nation ceases to be short of manpower and achieves an optimum balance or when it exceeds that level. During the early period of American economic development and until comparatively recent years we have experienced various degrees of labor shortages. A deficiency of manpower held down the rate of economic expansion. During the decade of the thirties, however, and up to the time of our full participation in the war, we have appeared to be suffering from an excess of manpower.

In a restricted sense, perhaps it could be said that the optimum size of the labor force had been at least temporarily exceeded. The existence of protracted large-scale unemployment, however, does not necessarily signify an overabundant labor supply in any functional sense. Factors quite unrelated to the size of the population, but deriving from specific institutional and market maladjustments of the type earlier described, may create the impression that the optimum labor force has been exceeded. In an economic environment such as obtained in the thirties, additions to the working population could not be expected to be readily absorbed—that is, unless changes in prevailing wage rates facilitated such a development.

Is there a reasonable presumption that an enlarged labor supply would affect supply and demand schedules so as to provoke a general

[36] There was a widespread practice in the past for immigrants to live with relatives in this country upon arrival or to "double up" with other newcomers; this reduces the initial impact from this source.

reduction for various classes of wage rates, increasing thereby the demand for labor? This view would appear to be plausible at first sight, especially since immigrant labor could be counted upon to accept wages below the levels to which native-born workers have been accustomed. Such a development, however, can be predicated only on the assumption of a relatively fluid supply—demand relationship unaffected by such institutional rigidities as are imposed by labor unions, government minimum-wage and maximum-hour laws, and so forth.[37] As evidence of the reality of institutional factors, witness the substantial gains in wage rates in numerous industries in the years 1935–1937 and later, during a period of rising business activity, but, nevertheless, characterized by great unemployment. Of course, had the federal government not instituted its relief and public works programs and had it hindered the organizational efforts of unions instead of lending tacit and frequently direct support, wage rates would probably not have made such appreciable gains.

If real wages were reduced as a consequence of a wave of new immigrant labor, cheaper production costs could, if translated into reduced selling prices, encourage demand and contribute to strengthening the recovery movement. Granted that some stimulus might be realized from this area, this is not the line of analysis adopted by Professor Hansen,[38] whose argument concentrates upon the consequent reduction of *extensive* consumer demand for durable and semi-luxury commodities.

A declining birth rate is a phenomenon associated with culturally advanced, industrialized countries enjoying relatively high standards of living.[39] The desire to protect prevailing standards of well-being, including savings, is consciously expressed through voluntary limitation of the size of the family. Expansion of demand for durable consumer goods (and consequently durable producer goods) has become increasingly a function of a rising standard of living or *intensive* consumer demand as opposed to the more characteristically extensive growth of demand attributable to population increase in earlier decades. Even in the past, however, the rise in the American standard of

[37] It is highly improbable, furthermore, that protective legislation would not be enacted to safeguard native-born workers from a surge of competition by foreign workers.

[38] Rather, the advantages of wage reductions as an implement for recovery are specifically denied.

[39] Except in countries in which the national government aggressively pursues a high birthrate policy through monetary inducements, tax penalties, propaganda, and so forth.

living has been responsible for a good portion of the total increase in economic activity. According to Willford I. King, the standard of living in the United States rose approximately 300 percent to 400 percent in the years from 1850 to 1928.[40] Conscious reduction of the birth rate has not reduced the demand for consumers' capital goods, but rather has made possible the insistent demand for a wide variety of consumers' durable goods which would otherwise have remained dormant.

As has frequently been observed, the representative American standard of living, even at this late date, is deplorably low despite the great gains over earlier decades. There existed in the prewar period virtually inexhaustible unsatisfied demand for a wide variety of consumers' durable and semiluxury goods, demand which would find increasing expression at higher-income levels.[41] The pertinence of repeated references to the potential demands of babes yet unborn may be questioned in a society in which there exist vast ungratified demands for necessities by the existing population.

INVESTMENT OPPORTUNITIES AND THE LIMITS OF ECONOMIC PENETRATION

The third major element in Professor Hansen's analysis of the factors responsible for economic progress is the stimulus derived from the "discovery and development of new territory and new resources."

It is not possible, I think, to make even an approximate estimate of the proportion of the new capital created in the nineteenth century which was a direct consequence of the opening up of new territory. . . . The opening of new territory and the growth of population were together responsible for a very large fraction—possibly somewhere near one-half of the total volume of new capital formation in the nineteenth century. These outlets for new investment are rapidly being closed. The report on Limits of Land Settlement by Isaiah Bowman and others may be regarded as conclusive in its findings that there are no important areas left for exploitation and settlement . . . no one is likely to challenge the statement that foreign investment will in the next fifty years play an incomparably smaller role than was the case in the nineteenth century.[42]

[40] This result is obtained by adding the improvement registered in per capita income for the period 1850 to 1910 as shown by Dr. King in *The Wealth and Income of the People of the United States*, Table XXI, p. 129, to the progress realized in the period 1909 to 1928 as revealed in Dr. King's subsequent study *The National Income and Its Purchasing Power*, Table XII, p. 87. These estimates are, of course, very rough.

[41] To the above items of unsatisfied demands must be added the demand for more security via more savings.

[42] "Progress and Declining Population," *American Economic Review*, XXIX (March, 1939), 9.

While some opportunity is seen to exist for industrialization of undeveloped areas, Professor Hansen does not think this job will be performed through capital export from mature industrial countries.

The analysis undertaken by Professor Hansen of the role played by economic penetration into undeveloped areas in the past and the consequences of the termination of this source of economic progress on the rate of capital formation is subject to the criticism already levied against his treatment of technological innovation and the growth of population. Hansen's conclusions are based again almost exclusively upon a consideration of external factors (ex post facto) unrelieved by an examination of related institutional and market phenomena and obscured by the absence of any definition of economic penetration.

Hansen stresses the disappearance of the frontier, although no date is submitted marking this event. Officially, that is, according to the United States Census Bureau, the frontier disappeared in 1880 with the announcement that the unsettled area had been "so broken into by isolated bodies of settlement that there can hardly be said to be a frontier line." [43] This definition is not adopted by Professor Hansen, who apparently believes that the frontier, in an economic sense, did not disappear until several decades later.

Unfortunately, the precise character of the transformation and the approximate date of its realization are not specified. Economic penetration is not treated as a qualitative concept meaningful only in relation to the prevailing stage of development of the arts. It is not, moreover, viewed as dependent upon the current economic environment and specific policies pursued with respect to the exploitation of the economic opportunities believed to reside in relatively uncultivated areas.

Hansen's apparition of technological saturation here assumes the closely allied guise of geographic saturation. We are not persuaded that the one is more real than the other. Surely, the opportunities for profitable investment in certain lines may for particular sections or even widespread areas of our economy become temporarily exhausted. The duration of this condition will depend upon the sum total of the numerous factors earlier described which in their interaction comprise the business environment. The reassertion of new investment will not be obliged to await the discovery of heathen terrain un-

---

[43] Turner, "The Significance of the Frontier in American History," address delivered at the State Historical Society of Wisconsin, *Forty-First Annual Meeting*, December 14, 1893, p. 1.

CRITIQUE OF SECULAR-STAGNATION 65

touched by technological development, but rather upon the correction of the specific market, institutional and psychological features responsible for the decline.

The extension of a spur line by a railroad should not be interpreted as the ultimate penetration of a given region. Measured in the light of the huge resources of this nation, the available economic opportunities have only begun to be tapped. Assuming any approximation to an optimum economic environment, we must admit that the economic frontier, far from being saturated, has no more than been surveyed.

With respect to Hansen's appraisal of the realization of the near limits to economic penetration beyond the confines of the United States proper, we submit the same argument that is presented above. Moreover, we venture to predict that in the first decade following the successful termination of World War II more American funds (both private and public) will be invested in foreign lands than were invested in the nineteen twenties or in the several decades prior to World War I.

Neither the United States nor the countries to which this nation extended loans (especially during the prosperity decade of the 1920's) derived any long-run advantages from these operations. The immediate impact of American foreign loans in the nine years 1921–1929 was to stimulate this country's export trade by an additional three and one-half billion dollars.[44] These purchases constituted a relatively unimportant source of demand. The failure of the United States, however, to purchase a sufficient volume of merchandise from the borrowing countries to permit the repayment of these obligations contributed substantially to international economic instability. This nation's protective tariff policy deprived our debtors of the ability to make repayment as well as the capacity to meet the interest obligations on the outstanding debt.[45]

In summary, Hansen's explanation submitted for the stagnation of the thirties is rejected. His doctrine, while directing attention to some of the more outstanding developments of recent decades, attributes to them a causal role which is at best spurious. The stagnation doctrine, reflecting the pervasive pessimism of the period in which it was born, seeks an explanation in terms of "fundamental underlying secu-

[44] Madden, Nadler, and Sauvain, *America's Experience as a Creditor Nation*, p. 84. See Chapter V for an analysis of the economic effects of capital exports.
[45] An analysis of defaults on foreign loans is contained in Chapter VI–VII, *ibid.*

lar phenomena" while ignoring frequently the consequences of more immediate considerations which make up the business environment. In effect, he dismisses the idea that cyclical fluctuations and short-run disequilibria and maladjustments are our central problems (developments susceptible in varying degree to external controls) and directs our attention instead to long-run developments (invariably unsusceptible to controls).

Thus, proposals for public policy are largely restricted to the public sector of the economy, the private sector, unfortunately, not being eligible for redemption. Under Hansen's analysis compensatory fiscal policy becomes the main vehicle for a high-income level, while under the alternative approach suggested fiscal policy constitutes but a single element in a complex program for achieving fuller utilization of resources.

We shall return to the latter problem in Chapter VIII. In the following chapter we undertake an analysis of the public debt problem, with an examination of Hansen's position as our point of departure. We shall seek to define the extent to which debt limitations restrict the scope of fiscal operations.

V. THE LIMITS TO PUBLIC DEBT

HISTORICALLY [Hansen points out] opposition to public debt . . . gradually broke down by reason of exigencies which appeared more or less uncontrollable . . . state borrowing entered as a by-product mainly of the increasingly costly outlays incident to modern warfare. It was not a question of theoretical principles but of practical, hard necessities. The tradition against borrowing was set aside, when grave emergencies, such as wars, forced the issue.[1]

Hansen seeks to depose the theoretical arguments and popular prejudice against public debt and utilize the borrowing power of the state as a mechanism for securing fuller utilization of resources. Deficit financing need not be limited to the support of military operations, but can be used as well for constructive peacetime activities. Hansen, throwing off the bonds of orthodox budgetary doctrine, contends that "public debt is an instrument of public policy. It is a means to control the national income and, in conjunction with the tax structure, to regulate the distribution of income." [2]

While Hansen's views on debt are integrally related to the secular-stagnation thesis, the doctrines presented have independent significance and stature of their own. If valid, his position involves not only a revolution in conventional federal budgetary practice, but opens, as well, a new orientation in the relation of government to the private sector of the economy.

Hansen contends (1) that an internally held public debt need not entail an economic burden and (2) that we need not be concerned over the imminence of reaching a ceiling on the national debt. Neither of these contentions is particularly novel. The latter proposition, however, as developed by Hansen, contains far-reaching implications; several of them, unfortunately, are not pursued.

With respect to the problem of evaluating the burden incidental to an internally held debt, Hansen points out that the answer depends (a) upon the character of the tax structure and (b) upon the objects of public expenditures. In so far as there exists an identity between the taxpayer and the bondholder, all that is involved is an accounting

[1] *Fiscal Policy and Business Cycles*, p. 135.   [2] *Ibid.*, p. 185.

transaction. No burden may be said to be entailed under such circumstances. In effect, however, the generally nonprogressive tax structures of the United States [3] and most European nations have involved a very real burden for the low-income groups, although Hansen seeks to disprove or to minimize this fact. The living standards of the mass of the population have been lowered by reason of the interest burden they have been obliged to bear. The internal transfer of funds to bondholders has been prejudicial to the over-all propensity to consume. Hansen's tax proposals, however, would contribute to minimizing the burden involved.

Our tax laws have, until very recently, tended to enforce an actual dichotomy, in the above sense, between taxpayers and bondholders. The tax-exemption privilege conferred upon holders of government bonds has operated to concentrate these issues in the hands of persons in the higher-income brackets. The popular distribution of war bonds during World War II will tend to reduce the real debt burden. However, since bond sales to the general public represent but a fraction of total war debt, cancellation of tax payments by government bond yields will be very incomplete.[4] In the postwar period it is not unlikely that a considerable redistribution of war bonds (via refunding and sale), comparable to World War I experience, may occur.

The burden entailed by a given magnitude of public debt will depend in part upon the objects of the expenditure. Mrs. U. K. Hicks [5] has created a useful classification of debt based upon the general character of public outlay, namely, (1) dead-weight debt, (2) passive debt, and (3) active debt. The first category refers to debt arising from expenditures not yielding any money return or future flow of utilities; the most prominent example of this type is war outlays. The second class refers to projects, such as parks, and so forth, which result in the creation of utilities, although no money income or gain in productivity (in the narrow sense) is involved. Debt arising from relief outlays must be included in the second category. This calls for a further distinction between maintenance and improvement or extension. The final category comprehends self-liquidating expenditures which di-

---

[3] Total tax levies, federal, state, and local combined, are non-progressive below incomes of $10,000. See United States, Temporary National Economic Committee, Monograph No. 3, *Who Pays the Taxes?* by Colm and Tarasov, p. 6.

[4] Hansen suggests that the large bond holdings of savings and financial institutions operate to the advantage of the numerous members thereof. The writer is somewhat doubtful of the premise.

[5] *The Finance of British Government, 1920–1936.*

THE LIMITS TO PUBLIC DEBT 69

rectly enhance the productivity of the nation. Dead-weight debt, as the name suggests, enjoys no compensating returns. The largest portion of outstanding national debt—for United States as well as the rest of the world—is of this type, having arisen out of war expenditures. With respect to this nation, the federal deficits incurred during the depression of the thirties represent the chief exception to the above rule.[6]

Deficits arising out of expenditures made for productive purposes (whether self-liquidating or otherwise) enhance the real wealth of the community and directly or indirectly augment the nation's taxable capacity. Certain projects (such as, for example, the Panama Canal) may result in enormous expansion of tax revenue and, in effect, entail no burden upon the economy as a whole. It is necessary to distinguish between the consequences for the economy as a whole and the impact upon different segments of society. The measure of the burden sustained by particular individuals or various income groups will depend upon an appraisal of the benefits conferred by certain expenditures as against the taxes attributable to same.

The third major determinant affecting the burden entailed by public debt relates to the effect of the expenditures so financed upon the level of employment and the standard of living. Hansen directs attention to the need for appraising the primary and secondary repercussions of deficit financing upon the national income. For even in the event that public debt imposes unfavorably upon the consumption stream, the long-run effects may outweigh this disadvantage. Hansen underscores the favorable effects of the relatively concentrated ownership of the enormous dead-weight British debt in the nineteenth century upon English industry.[7] The regressive tax structure of Britain during that century, it is claimed, served to augment the volume of savings so vital in a period characterized by rapid industrial expansion. Moreover, Hansen also suggests that the high level of British public debt after World War I was, in retrospect, a favorable development. For in this period, given the prevailing progressive tax structure and the relatively wide dispersal of debt holdings, it may have contributed to stimulating the consumption level.[8] This shift, Hansen claims, fortunately coincided with the need for favoring the con-

---
[6] State and local government debt has, of course, been assumed very largely for productive and utility-creating projects.

[7] *Fiscal Policy and Business Cycles*, pp. 153-157.

[8] It is debatable whether statistical evidence could be submitted to support this contention.

sumption stream relative to the flow of savings. Professor Hansen's recommendations (1) that deficit financing be utilized as a means of assuring fuller utilization of resources, (2) with expenditures devoted to productive projects and (3) that the tax system be designed in such fashion that the debt burden is minimized, are calculated to postpone indefinitely the realization of an intolerable level of public debt. As previously indicated, Hansen is not entirely clear with respect to the factors establishing the limits to public indebtedness.[9] He appears to waver between a debt limit established (1) primarily by the Treasury's ability to meet current interest payments on outstanding debt [10]— a relatively conventional criterion—and (2) a limit determined preeminently by considerations relating to the avoidance of inflation [11] —a very different type of orientation.

In connection with the former limitation Hansen stresses the flexibility of taxable capacity. Despite the importance of this consideration to the entire compensatory fiscal program, Professor Hansen unfortunately fails to discuss some of the more significant variables involved. An attempt in this direction is accordingly made here.

The limits to taxation are, for the most part, more tangible than those governing debt. The former can be expressed largely in terms of incentive,[12] while the latter is dependent upon such factors as were indicated above as well as the prevailing institutional framework. Highly progressive personal and corporate income taxes clearly reduce the incentives to business enterprise.[13] In the event of an increase in the rates of both personal and corporate income taxes, the burden will be especially onerous because of the element of double taxation involved. The sharper tax schedules called for by Hansen will particularly discourage all types of enterprise involving more than a moderate degree of risk. The attraction of possible substantial gains is vitiated by the certain obligation of surrendering a large portion of the returns to the federal Treasury. In effect, the gambling odds are lengthened. Business innovators (Schumpeter's pioneer) would be particularly adversely effected. While less discouragement would re-

[9] See *ibid.*, pp. 168 ff.
[10] "As long as the interest on the public debt is well within the practical taxable capacity of the government, taking the entire business cycle into consideration . . . no question can arise with respect to the solvency of the government." *Ibid.*, p. 159.
[11] *Ibid.*, pp. 175–185.
[12] See the discussion of tax capacity contained in the Twentieth Century Fund, *Facing the Tax Problem*, pp. 57–68.
[13] We shall return to this problem in Chapter VIII.

THE LIMITS TO PUBLIC DEBT 71

sult in connection with safer types of business operations, increased tax levies will nevertheless exert an inhibiting impulse in this area, too, since the element of risk is present to some extent for virtually every type of business venture. The growth of the sentiment that "the game is not worth the candle" presents itself as a real threat long before confiscatory rates set in.[14] Advocates of the stagnation doctrine tend to ignore the problem of incentives as related to the tax program, perhaps in part due to their rather negative orientation toward private enterprise in general.

Hansen's tax proposals are primarily related to increasing the consumption stream or, to put it in another fashion, the propensity to consume function. Idle savings will accordingly be drained from the savings stream by a highly progressive income tax. Closely allied to this objective is the desire to reduce the prevalent inequalities in wealth and income.[15] The revenue function proper of the tax system is viewed as entirely subsidiary to the above considerations. Thus, we may be said to have arrived at a radical transformation of the conventional approach to the tax system. Taxation, in combination with planned deficit financing, is converted into an instrument designed to achieve fuller utilization of resources. The respective reliance placed upon taxation relative to public borrowing is declared to be a function of the needs of the prevailing economic picture.

In the above connection Hansen seems to reject the limitation upon indebtedness arising from the ability of the tax system to meet the interest payments on outstanding debt. This ceiling is apparently succeeded by another based entirely upon the requirements of the current business environment. The most tangible limit is the short-term limit arising from the need to forestall inflation. The specific debt level itself is presumably no cause for concern.

Hansen stresses the fact that there exist no fixed limits to public debt. The possibility of eliminating interest payments on public issues through the adoption of the "Hundred Percent Reserve Plan," or another type of program providing for the issuance of noninterest

[14] While it is true that the incentives to enterprise are in part institutional, not solely a function of the prospective rate of return, it would, indeed, be gratuitous to suggest that the drive for profit could be subordinated in favor of more general social ends.

[15] "To mitigate this inequality in wealth and income it is necessary to finance the large proportion of government expenditures from taxation. Indeed, this is the primary function of a steeply progressive tax structure. Were it not for the fact that a rapidly mounting debt tends toward wealth concentration, borrowing is always to be preferred to taxation, since borrowing is always a more expansionist method of financing expenditures." *Ibid.*, p. 179.

bearing notes, is rejected. Such a step is discouraged on the score that (1) the monetary supply may thus become excessive, (2) the interest rate would be driven to a very low level, and (3) the banks and other financial institutions would in consequence be deprived of a livelihood.[16] Hansen, in effect, removes concern over the debt level as a limitation upon the scope of governmental fiscal activities. The particular balance to be realized between tax revenue on the one hand and deficit financing on the other will be determined in accordance with the dictates of the prevailing economic scene.

The above conclusions, while they may be anathema to orthodox students of public finance, present an effective challenge to the classical budgetary tradition. Hansen contends that the fiscal rules inherited from earlier periods enjoying relative full utilization of resources are inappropriate for an economy suffering from protracted idle resources. The traditional aversion to the growth of public debt, based largely upon popular concern for the stability of government credit and fear of inflation, is rejected. Instead, the debt-incurring power of the state is to be utilized as a means of securing fuller employment of resources. The credit of the government need not be impaired, nor need we suffer the ravages of inflation in consequence. These problems, Hansen insists, are wholly manageable.

Hansen appears to weaken his argument by omitting a more detailed discussion of the means by which inflation is to be combated. He seems to assume that no appreciable price rise is likely until a condition of relative full employment is realized. Our wartime experience, however, has clearly established that inflation will not be postponed until the above point has been achieved, but may confront us long before that time, arising out of localized shortages and competition for resources.[17] In rejecting cyclically adjusted tax rates Hansen renounces perhaps the most effective instrument for defeating inflation. This decision stems from his tendency to assume, in approaching the future, that cyclical fluctuations will be of only negligible proportions as well as from the view that the permanent raising of the pro-

[16] It is interesting to note that we have been drifting in the above direction for some years prior to the war. Our monetary supply has become very abundant, although this development has not precipitated inflation. The decline in the interest rate, especially for short-term issues, has to an extent already operated to produce the results predicted above.

[17] An important distinction, of course, between periods of war and peace is the fact that the time element is of paramount importance in the former case and hence produces an exaggerated and intensified pressure upon prices.

pensity to consume is of greater importance than any effort to reduce cyclical fluctuations.[18]

The alternative device of curtailing public expenditures in the face of an inflationary threat is likely to be far less expeditious. For one thing, as earlier observed, various types of outlay cannot readily be terminated. Of perhaps greater importance is the fact that the secondary repercussions attendant to a given volume of public outlay cannot be satisfactorily gauged in advance. The problem posed by the above considerations is of profound importance. For, following Hansen's prescription, we are obliged to dwell either in imminent danger of inflation or else reduce the scope of the government's spending program by way of tolerating a moderate amount of unemployed resources.

The adoption of the above perspective toward public debt may entail a corollary extension of controls over the money markets, banks, and other financial institutions to assure successful execution of the borrowing program envisaged. While the huge current holdings of government issues by all financial institutions virtually compel continued subscription to new series, lest their present commitments be exposed to a reduction in value, additional safeguards in this direction may be desirable. The banking system may have to be oriented more closely to the Treasury's needs and a greater measure of control extended over the lending practices pursued.

Hansen's proposals do such violence to orthodox budgetary views, as well as to popular prejudice, that it appears of some worth to appraise the general character of the problems involved in public debt.

THE RELATIVITY OF PUBLIC DEBT

The literature on public finance in the English classical tradition is replete with cautions against incurring debt. The opposition to public debt was, in part, based upon the demonstrated weaknesses of earlier monetary systems, the fear of inflation, debt repudiation, and so forth. While state and local governments in this country have long followed the practice of borrowing for self-liquidating capital improvements, the national government (whose scope for self-liquidating investment has been comparatively limited) has traditionally, albeit unsuccessfully, sought to combat a progressive extension of public debt. With the general exception of wartime periods and the unique

[18] *Ibid.*, p. 298.

development of the decade of the thirties,[19] the federal government has tended to observe the above rule.

The great expansion of public debt during the thirties prompted dire fear in numerous quarters over the consequences of this unprecedented peacetime phenomenon. Our newly discovered proclivity to assume debt has both surprised and dismayed the American populace. To the extent to which the average citizen is concerned with such elusive problems as the public debt and its manifold implications, he still appears to cling to the analogy of private to public debt, with the associated obligation of relating peacetime borrowing to the creation of self-liquidating assets. The question concerning the extent to which the pyramiding of public debt can proceed has repeatedly been raised. The more conventional measures establishing the economic significance and burden imposed by public debt are expressed in relation to such considerations as: (1) the size of the national income; (2) the ratio of interest payments on the debt to national income; (3) per capita debt load; and (4) the comparative debt statistics and ratios of the United States and foreign experience. In a sense, however, all that such calculations and comparisons establish is our current position with respect to our or other nations' earlier experience. The ratio of public debt or interest payments to national income or wealth possesses no final significance in itself, nor does it necessarily indicate anything with respect to the future ability—or desirability—of incurring deficits.

In 1790 a federal debt of $72 million prompted considerable concern; in 1865 a debt of $2.75 billion raised dire fears over the capacity of our Treasury to carry this burden; in 1919 the rise of the national debt to $26.6 billion provoked serious financial apprehension. On a per capita basis federal debt rose from $3.00 in 1861, at the opening of the Civil War, to $75 in 1865, at the close of the war. In the three years between 1916 and 1919 federal debt multiplied more than twenty times and reached a level nearly ten times the Civil War figure. The large-scale borrowing prompted by the great depression brought the federal debt up from $16 billion at the end of 1930 to $40.4 billion at the end of 1939. Throughout the decade of the thirties there raged a bitter debate over the ability of the Treasury to support a burden of such magnitude. With the advent of World War II, however, all preceding debt figures fade in comparison. By the end of

[19] The indebtedness arising out of the depression was roughly equal to that resulting from World War I.

THE LIMITS TO PUBLIC DEBT

January, 1943, the federal debt had jumped to over $112 billion, with the fiscal year of 1944 likely to witness a rise to well over $200 billion. It is impossible to foretell to what level the debt will expand before hostilities cease. Prospective postwar foreign reconstruction loans will further augment the debt load. Thus the outlook for the next few years is for a progressive extension in the debt level.

The relativity of the debt problem is graphically illustrated by the marked contrast in the attitude manifested toward the debt incurred during the thirties for relief and public works as opposed to the obligations assumed in connection with the nation's war effort. The former type of borrowing was the object of violent attack from many quarters and national financial ruin was monotonously predicted as a consequence. On the other hand, in the face of a more concrete threat to our society in the shape of war, the uncertain and indeterminant fears surrounding the fate of public credit were largely dissipated. No one would hazard the suggestion that we could not *afford* to repel the invader. In wartime, financial considerations are subordinated very largely in favor of the physical problems of production and supply.[20]

National emergencies, such as war, which cut across party lines and domestic controversies tend to nullify conventional responses toward debt. The moment, however, that public outlays for such controversial purposes as unemployment relief, emergency public works, public power projects, and other developments which may compete with private enterprise are involved, the dangers surrounding a mounting public debt are advanced. To the extent to which the objects of peacetime public expenditure involve a redistribution of income favorable to the lower- and medium-income groups at the expense of the upper-income brackets, the opposition from this latter quarter is readily understandable. Frequently attacks against the incurrence of debt are not unrelated to political sabotage. Objections derived from other sources may more conveniently be expressed in terms of opposition to the incidental debt involved.

A fundamental concern with respect to public borrowing stems from the expectation that future tax rates will have to be increased to meet the resultant interest burden. This belief detracts strongly from whatever attraction public borrowing might possess as an alternative to an immediate rise in tax rates. In consequence, public resistance to uninterrupted pyramiding of national debt stiffens as current tax im-

[20] See the article "The Humbug of Finance," *London Economist*, CXL (May 3, 1941), 579–580.

positions become more onerous. The opposition engendered by activities financed by borrowing will be a function, in part, of the character of the prevailing tax structure. The greater the reliance placed upon a markedly progressive tax structure, the more vociferous will be the opposition of the groups affected.

Borrowing is always less painful (initially at least) than taxation. A bond issue of $10 billion can be serviced by annual interest charges of $250 million (at 2.5 percent). Thus, taxpayers are $9,750,000,000 better off the first year than under a pay-as-you-go basis. In the event that the interest charges are placed entirely upon the subscribers to the new issue no tax burden, in a nominal sense, is involved. However, alternative uses for the funds may have been sacrificed. Capital may have been transferred from promising investment fields to areas where the stimulus to production is less. This latter proposition may be used, perhaps, as an argument against making the expenditure. But, if the expenditure is to be made, the initial impact of borrowing upon the tax bill will always be less onerous than full financing out of current revenue.

If borrowing is so much less painful than tax financing, why oppose deficit financing? Even in the event that tax levies are imposed upon groups who do not hold federal issues, is not the burden less than that entailed in balancing the budget? The specific burden for different income groups, as already indicated, will depend upon the character of the tax system on the one hand and the objects of expenditure on the other. From the viewpoint of the tax burden upon the economy as a whole, however, is not borrowing much more attractive than the alternate? The answer, for the short-run, is an unequivocal "yes" for periods other than those enjoying relative full employment. But what of the long-run picture? Are there debt limits beyond which a society may no longer resort to borrowing with impunity?

It has generally been contended that limits do exist, however difficult to estimate, to the public debt a society can sustain. B. V. Ratchford, for example, states:

When we choose to remove a monetary obstacle to present production or to finance a war by creating a debt, we are able to do so because we have freedom of action. But by that act we give hostages to the future; we restrict our freedom of action to deal with new problems which may arise and at the same time create an obstacle which, according to the best of our knowledge at present, will be a chronic economic problem.[21]

[21] "The Burden of a Domestic Debt," *American Economic Review*, XXXII (September, 1942), 467.

THE LIMITS TO PUBLIC DEBT 77

Mr. Ratchford stresses the inhibiting consequences of a rising tax burden upon the incentives to new private investment. But is it not true that the current tax bill will have to be greatly augmented if deficits are to be eliminated? Thus, current tax levels may immediately present the hazards of future, heavier tax rates.

The avoidance of increased tax burdens can be achieved only by a reduction of expenditures. Increased burdens upon enterprise can be evaded, in part, by shifting a heavier tax burden to the consumption stream. But, properly speaking, the distribution of the tax burden is an entirely different issue. Unless we assume a stable or declining level of national income, the real tax burden for the economy as a whole should be reduced by a borrowing program. An increased income means that a given interest burden will represent a declining portion of the national dividend. An interest burden of $2 billion, with a national income of $150 billion, presents a smaller burden, *cateris paribus*, than an interest charge of the same magnitude with an income of $120 billion. The public debt represents a declining burden so long as national income rises relatively faster than interest charges.

But what of the mechanical obstacles to protracted accumulation of public debt? Can the banks support any further great expansion of debt? Can such expansion materialize without producing serious inflation? Professor Angell [22] replies in the affirmative to both of these questions.

As long as the Federal government retains its present direct and indirect powers over the currency supply, the Federal Reserve Banks, the money markets and hence even over the commercial banking system, there can be no serious mechanical obstacle to very large further increases in the Federal debt, and (if the increases are not made too abruptly) at low rates of interest.[23]

Public spending during periods suffering substantial idle resources counteracts the increase in "effective" hoards. New government issues, by absorbing individual or corporate hoards or increasing bank deposits, in the event of sales to such institutions, tend to place in circulation funds which firms and individuals do not choose to spend. The increase in money stock occurring "is not in itself a dangerous development, for the expansion really takes place merely in order to enable certain groups to increase their holdings of idle cash *without* thereby bringing about any substantial and enduring decrease in na-

[22] *Investment and Business Cycles*, pp. 242-256.   [23] *Ibid.*, pp. 242-243.

tional money income or in the total volume of employment." [24]

In the event of a rapid general decline in the level of liquidity preferences, a surge of corporate and individual spending may, if combined with large-scale federal spending, bring about a condition of temporary commodity shortages and consequently price inflation. Such a development took place during the second half of 1936 and the early part of 1937. A prompt and appreciable increase in reserve requirements obliging a reduction in commercial bank loans and other portfolio holdings should help to counteract such movements, though if overdone it may precipitate a recession. The failure of the Federal Reserve authorities to adopt a more rigorous counterinflationary policy in 1936 and 1937 explains in part the relatively meager results achieved. An intelligently timed federal spending program, involving a tapering off of expenditures during a period of rapidly rising activity is a necessary corollary to restrictive central bank policy.

The experience of the above period, which culminated in the fall recession of 1937, illustrates graphically the problem of controlling violent short-run price and economic fluctuations. While short-run business behavior will always present serious difficulties of control, the problems involved in long-term inflation are eminently subject to central controls. As earlier indicated, the existence of a cyclically adjustable tax program is an indispensable complementary device to monetary technics of control.

Professor Seymour E. Harris [25] has contemplated with equanimity a rise in federal debt to $4,000 billion in the next fifty or sixty years. Such a debt level, involving some $80 billion annual interest payments, could be supported, he contends, out of a national income of $200 billion, exclusive of interest on public debt. The total tax bill, including nondebt outlay, would amount to a hypothetical sum of $115 billion. The real tax burden, however, will be far less than the preceding figure, since, it is held, taxes assessed for transfer payments are less burdensome than nontransfer payments.

While Harris's arithmetic is somewhat obscure [26] and his conclusions as to the ability of carrying a debt of such proportions with a national income, *exclusive* of interest charges, of $200 billion are not at all established in detail, the more general argument presented appears to be well founded. That is:

[24] *Ibid.*, pp. 244–245.   [25] See *Postwar Economic Problems*, chap. x.
[26] See *ibid.*, p. 184.

THE LIMITS TO PUBLIC DEBT

Accumulation of debt will not bring ultimate collapse if the economy continues to grow. Tax capacity increases with the rise in income; and so long as the rise of debt charges is kept well within the limits set by a rising trend of income and capacity to pay taxes, no fears need be felt concerning a rising public debt. But a continued rise of the cost of debt in the face of stable or, even worse, falling incomes will ultimately bring disaster.[27]

The fact of the matter appears to be that if private investment cannot secure relatively full employment, public outlays will be demanded to fill the unemployment gap. It is highly unlikely that consideration for principles of "sound" finance can compete with the political pressure for governmental action. If the latter proposition proves to be correct, it will be of primary importance to develop institutional safeguards and technics for accommodating an increased volume of public debt with a minimum of disturbance.

As the level of national debt increases proposals for eliminating interest payments on federal issues will receive more careful consideration than hitherto has been the case. The replacement of interest-bearing bonds held by financial institutions by 100 percent reserve banking notes, noninterest-bearing and nonterminable obligations, would eliminate the entire problem of debt burden.[28] That is, new currency would be created to finance deficits. An excessive money supply would be combated by absorbing the reserves created by the new currency. The adoption of such a program would, of course, revolutionize our entire banking structure. Commercial banks would no longer play a central role in determining the flow of funds to business. Furthermore, the banks, deprived of their main source of income, would probably be succeeded by new institutions supported by charges placed on checking accounts and other banking services. If expansionist public spending becomes the chief vehicle for combating underutilization of resources, the federal debt may rise so rapidly in the postwar years as to lend the 100 percent reserve plan an irresistible attraction.

Much apprehension over the superannuation of orthodox budgetary criteria arises from the belief that once the simple and safe rules requiring a balanced budget are scrapped, they cannot be supplanted with a set of equally authoritative criteria. The answer lies in the fact that the program proposed by Hansen calls for a great shift of re-

[27] *Ibid.*, pp. 170–171.
[28] See Frank Graham, "Partial Reserve Money and the One Hundred Per Cent Proposal," *American Economic Review*, XXVI (September, 1936), 428–440.

sponsibility to the federal government. The revised budgetary rules would be governed by the necessity of assuring a condition of relatively full employment. Consequently they cannot enjoy the same simple nature that characterized traditional budgetary policy. The results achieved will depend upon the intelligence with which the program is implemented and the effectiveness of the safety valves adopted.

PUBLIC DEBT AND THE THREAT TO PRIVATE ENTERPRISE

Granting the feasibility of a considerable extension of public debt, the question of the consequent repercussions upon the system of private enterprise is forcibly raised. Henry C. Simons, in appraising the implications of Hansen's recommendations,[29] maintains that public investment proceeding with unlimited funds will raise interest costs to the private sector of the economy, compete for funds and resources with private enterprise, increase the costs of capital assets through governmental competition, and add its interest burden to tax charges. Professor Simons further contends that Hansen's proposals create an environment in which private enterprise and government-socialized enterprise confront each other in uninterrupted bitter battle, with the government inevitably tending toward absolutism.

While Simons's contention that compensatory fiscal policy spells the disintegration of free exchange and free enterprise is very much on the lurid side and he underestimates the vitality of private enterprise as well as the good will and intelligence of our legislators (and bureaucrats), the problem posed is not entirely fictitious. Assuming adoption of Hansen's program, the actual conflict realized will be determined very largely by the spirit in which the government's plan is prosecuted. Hansen himself would certainly insist upon executing the program in a fashion (and in proportions) least likely to prejudice the interests and prospects of private enterprise. The demarcation of the proper sphere for public outlays, provided that this left ample scope for a variable program, should help to solve the above problem.[30]

Unfortunately Hansen does not address himself to the very important set of problems involved in establishing the sphere of public, relative to private activity, the issue of public competition with pri-

[29] In his article "Hansen on Fiscal Policy," *Journal of Political Economy*, L (April, 1942), 192.
[30] This problem will be further investigated in Chapter VII.

vate enterprise (or the threat of such activity), or the effect upon private costs of large-scale public operations over a wide range of activity. Hansen is primarily occupied in investigating the public side of the dual economy equation to which reference is made. The all-important consideration of the nature of the impact of the expanded scope of public enterprise upon private activity is not recognized to be a problem. This deficiency robs Hansen's analysis of an element of realism which does much to undermine the value of his recommendations.

It is impossible to predict whether or not Hansen's fiscal proposals will culminate in socializing large sectors of our economy—as Simons warns. Hansen's recommendations are so general that much would depend upon the specific implementation adopted. While we have rejected Hansen's secular-stagnation doctrine, we have found more validity in parts of his analysis of the significance and potential utility of public debt. We are persuaded that, within limits, deficit financing can be utilized as a mechanism for increasing the level of national income. Unlike Hansen, however, we are not attracted to a monistic solution based exclusively upon the exploitation of the state's spending authority. Attributing the prolonged depression to specific institutional and psychological maladjustments, we are inclined to insist upon the direct confrontation and adjustment of these problems themselves. This viewpoint will be presented in some detail in Chapter VIII.

While Hansen's analysis of the role of public debt proceeds almost entirely upon a purely economic level, some concession to popular prejudice on the subject is made by way of championing the cause of the capital-current budget system. As previously observed, the design of the budgetary accounting system is a relatively subsidiary issue, subordinate to the more basic decision establishing the scope of government investment and spending operations. Compensatory fiscal policy is not at all dependent upon the adoption of a capital-current budget but may be pursued without any such separation of accounts.

Underlying the advocacy of a capital-current budget rests the eminently practical objective of combating popular apprehension surrounding a progressive rise in national debt. Public concern is to be assuaged through the identification of debt with durable capital projects. A relatively elaborate accounting system becomes the sugar-coating disguising the bitter debt pill. The new budgetary orthodoxy would be observed as long as interest charges on capital outlays were regularly met out of current revenue.

There can be no dispute over the mere accounting function performed by a capital-current budget.[31] Distinguishing between these two types of outlay is useful in revealing the true character of fiscal operations during the year. Lumping capital and current expenditures together, in effect, obscures Treasury policy and activity. Huge deficits, concentrated in a single year or in several years, incurred for capital projects with life spans of several decades, create a false picture of spending activity. This is true of self-liquidating, as well as nonremunerative investment. The capital account may or may not lump the latter category along with the former.[32]

It is pertinent to indicate that the adoption of a capital-current budget will not necessarily reduce the size of the deficit below what would have prevailed under a unitary accounting system. For if capital outlays under a dual budget were maintained at a relatively constant level over a number of years, the annual interest charges thus required would tend to approach a sum equal to that involved were capital operations financed on a current basis.[33] Only in the event of a marked increase in public investment or else highly erratic capital outlays would the current budgetary balance be improved.

The distinction in the financing methods prescribed for capital investment as opposed to current operations (borrowing as against support out of current revenue) may strain the not-always-too-clear distinction between these two types of activity. Deficits which threaten to materialize as a result of current activity could be avoided by shifting certain classes of expenditure to the capital account. Thus, for example, direct relief expenditures could be transferred from the current to the capital account (in the event that no distinction was made between self-liquidating and nonself-liquidating outlay) by instituting some form of work relief, without regard for the value of projects undertaken.

[31] See Erik Lindahl's excellent discussion in his *Studies in the Theory of Money and Capital*, Appendix, "The Problem of Balancing the Budget."

[32] Swedish budgetary procedure distinguishes between self-liquidating and nonself-liquidating capital outlay including only the former in the capital account. Danish practice, however, dispenses with this separation and accords identical treatment to both types of expenditure. See the description of the Swedish program by Gunnar Myrdal, "The Swedish Budget," *Fortune*, XVIII (September, 1938), 65–66 and 130–145.

[33] Such industries as public light and power and other utilities, which undertake large, fairly continuous capital additions, find it advantageous to treat such outlays as current in character.

THE LIMITS TO PUBLIC DEBT

As already indicated, the revised budgetary system is largely designed to reduce popular concern over the rise in public debt. How effective is this device likely to be? Since no propaganda monopoly has been conferred upon advocates of a capital-current budget, there is small prospect that wholesale conversion will be achieved through this medium.

The groups most energetically opposed to peacetime deficit financing, namely, the largest segment of the press and organized business groups, have hotly attacked the foregoing budgetary proposal. As far as the focal point for most of the cross-firing propaganda is concerned —the man in the street—the inability of alleged authorities to achieve any agreement in this entire field has probably accomplished no more than add to his confusion. The truth of the matter seems to be that the problem of fiscal policy is quite distantly removed from association with tangible accounting rules and lies instead in the limbo of political, economic and social expediency in which area concise criteria evade us.

The limits to public debt may be reduced largely to considerations of taxable capacity. A tax burden becomes excessive when it entails a drain upon current personal and corporate incomes serious enough to effect a reduction of production. The taxable capacity of an economy is, of course, a variable factor, depending upon the size of the national dividend, its distribution, the character of the tax structure, and other such considerations. While taxes on surpluses may increase the marginal propensity to consume, such levies at the same time serve to reduce the marginal efficiency of capital and hence the incentives to new investment. Unfortunately, the multiplicity of factors surrounding entrepreneurial behavior is such as to make most difficult the appraisal of the precise consequences of a given increase in taxes bearing upon business income. It is very difficult, as well, to judge the effects on national income of a given withdrawal from the consumption stream as opposed to the savings and investment flow. The answer will vary considerably over a period of time, with changes in the business setting. Any analysis of the impact of additional direct tax levies must rest upon certain assumptions with respect to the slopes of the supply and demand schedules for new investment.[34]

The burden imposed by the revenue system may be separated into transfer payments, or charges on the public debt, on the one hand and

[34] See Angell, *Investment and Business Cycles*, pp. 276–277.

nontransfer or regular expenditures on the other. Transfer charges will always constitute a smaller burden than that entailed by an equivalent sum levied to support ordinary, or nontransfer, expenditures. This must be true because of the fact that the groups supporting interest charges are to an extent also recipients of interest payments. Thus, if annual interest obligations are equal to regular, tax supported outlays, the burden of debt charges will always be lighter than that for the latter class of expenditures.

As far as the United States is concerned, the burden of supporting current activities has always been vastly greater than that obliged by debt service. Insofar as the total tax burden is held excessive at any given time, it could be argued to be the result of attempting to support too large a share of aggregate expenditures out of current revenue. More correctly, however, the rise in public expenditures at a pace faster than can be met currently by the prevailing taxable capacity indicates that the difficulty lies in the level of expenditures itself. If tax capacity falls behind the need for current revenue, public borrowing is a necessary and desirable means of postponing or averting the day of reckoning.

We have earlier noted the significance of the progressive rise in the tax burden upon enterprise as well as the total share of the national income captured by tax levies. There is little reason for believing this trend is likely to be reversed in the near future or even in the long run. Such a development would be contingent upon a reduction in total public expenditures (federal, state, and local) in the postwar years to a level comparable to prewar experience. This is very unlikely.[35] We are thus confronted with a problem of profound significance for the future of capitalist enterprise. Will excessive tax burdens eventually spell the doom of our economic institutions? We shall not presume to answer. It is pertinent, however, to note that public borrowing renders the great service of permitting us to escape the problem for the present and, in all likelihood, for some time to come. As long as national income increases more rapidly than the total tax burden, there is no great cause for alarm.

Perhaps, however, the problem of taxable capacity and the burden entailed by a rising public debt can be escaped by another route. As earlier described, the 100 percent reserve banking scheme would free us from the burdens of public indebtedness. While not enough is

[35] See pages 52 ff.

known of the operating details of such a program and perhaps many of the inherent dangers are unrecognized because of the general unfamiliarity with the proposal, it deserves serious examination as an adjunct to an economy laboring under current or prospective debt of excessive proportions.

VI. PUBLIC SPENDING, 1933-1940

THE PRESENT CHAPTER is devoted to an evaluation of the influence of Roosevelt fiscal and allied economic policy upon business activity in the period 1933-1940. Chapter VII will be concerned with establishing the more general significance of this experience, as well as appraising the scope and limitations of compensatory fiscal policy.

National economic policy in the years 1933-1940 was dominated by the exigencies of the depression-ridden decade. It is not strange that the successive economic measures of this period, born of dire necessity and nurtured by political and economic expediency, were characterized by inconsistency and improvisation. Inheriting an unprecedented obligation for economic leadership relinquished by private enterprise, the Roosevelt administration searched frantically for a formula capable of achieving recovery. With the conventional weapon of central banking policy repudiated, the New Deal was obliged to embark upon uncharted seas. The subsequent devious course traced was the inevitable route of the experimenter. Denied the security and guidance of precedent, the administration was torn between the need for innovation, organized resistance to change, and its own uncertainties over the policies adopted. The outcome, as must be the case under such circumstances, was something less than a consistent, articulate, and aggressive economic program.

The depression inherited from the Republican administration failed to exhibit a normal tendency toward recovery. A fundamental error of the Hoover administration was its tenacious view that the post-1929 collapse was merely another recession—long after its unprecedented severity had become apparent. Primary reliance upon banking policy, combined with desultory attempts at halting the deflationary spiral in progress, proved sorely inadequate as a means of terminating the economic decline. Every proposal to depart from conservative fiscal policy was denounced and used as an opportunity for reaffirming the validity of budgetary orthodoxy. All pleas for direct federal relief appropriations and allied demands were frustrated. The only significant deviation of the Hoover administration from its restrictive fiscal doctrine occurred in the salvaging loans of the Reconstruction Finance Corporation.

The Republican administration appeared to exalt the observance of fiscal orthodoxy—as personified by a balanced budget—above all other considerations. The deficits realized in the fiscal years 1931 and 1932 caused great alarm in official circles. In President Hoover's last budget address on December 5, 1932, he declared, with respect to the prospective deficit for the fiscal year 1933:[1]

> Such a situation cannot be continued without disaster to the Federal finances. . . . I cannot too strongly urge that every effort be made to limit expenditures and avoid additional obligations not only in the interest of the already heavily burdened taxpayer but in the interest of the very integrity of the finances of the Federal Government.[2]

It has been contended[3] that Hoover's anti-expansionist policies did, in effect, conquer the depression, rather than the measures of the succeeding administration. There is evidence for the belief that the incipient recovery in progress during the second half of 1932 might have continued had the rehabilitation of the banking structure been effected. For the American business revival in 1932 was no isolated phenomenon, but apparently a part of the general recovery then current among the principal European countries,[4] especially England. It would appear, however, that the American depression had proceeded to such depths that the prospects of a slow, gradual improvement were not sufficient to meet the requirements of an emergency situation. A "natural" recovery would have had to combat the deflationary spiral which, in some sectors of the economy, had not yet achieved its final resolution. There was small likelihood of sustained recovery in the face of a shaky banking structure, a huge volume of imminent farm and urban residential mortgage foreclosures, a seriously troubled agricultural situation, and a vast unemployment problem.

In restrospect it appears clear that economic developments during 1931 and 1932 were leading relentlessly in the direction of expanded federal fiscal operations—large outright relief and recovery outlays, as well as extended loan activities. The ever-growing legions of the unemployed demanding relief soon transcended the financial abilities

[1] Of the $6.3 billion deficit sustained in the fiscal years 1931–1933, slightly more than half is attributable to a reduction in tax receipts, the remainder, $2.9 billion or 46 percent is due to an increase of expenditures. This latter rise in outlay was the result largely of RFC and other loan operations.
[2] United States, President's Message Transmitting the Budget, December 5, 1932, p. xvii.
[3] See Schumpeter, *Business Cycles*, II, 984–985.
[4] See League of Nations, *World Economic Survey, 1935–1936*, p. 14.

of the local and state governments, supplemented by private charitable contributions. The weakened position of local and state treasuries soon impaired their ability to borrow the required funds. The persistent worsening of the condition of all classes of debtors and the prospects of ever greater waves of residential and farm mortgage foreclosures, bank runs, and business bankruptcies, created an economic environment which appeared to offer no prospect of early substantial improvement.

The numerous manifestations of social unrest, evident particularly in the ranks of the unemployed and in distressed agricultural regions, presented the most effective challenge to the prevailing fiscal policy. While a steadily growing chorus representing virtually every important group in our society was demanding some type or other of federal aid, it was the menacing rumblings of the unemployed and farmers that doomed the pleas of the budget-balancing school.

In the face of such powerful popular clamor, the conservative fiscal policies of the Hoover administration became politically untenable. Regardless of the candidate elected to the Presidency in 1932, an expansionist budgetary policy was inevitable.

It is interesting to speculate upon the extent to which the fiscal measures adopted by the New Deal after 1933 would have been duplicated by a Republican administration. There are many reasons for believing that the Republicans would have been obliged to extend their lending operations and embark upon a program of direct unemployment relief. The politics of democracy do not long tolerate the existence of a wide gulf between popular demands and administrative indulgence. However, it is highly improbable that a Republican administration would have engaged in a fiscal program comparable to that given expression by their Democratic successors. The conservative "antispending" disposition of the Republican party would have assured a minimum fiscal response. While the most urgent political demands would probably have been assuaged, it is not very likely that the pump-priming notion would have gained much support or that any compensatory investment policy would have been countenanced.

FROM THE INAUGURATION TO WPA

The Roosevelt victory in the electoral contest of November, 1932, represented not so much the triumph of a clearly formulated economic program as it did the popular repudiation of the policies of the Hoover administration. The recovery platform of Mr. Roosevelt gave little hint of what was to follow. Pre-election commitments, while promising prompt action on various fronts to stimulate economic recovery, followed the campaign tradition of safe generalities and left the administration uncommitted to any particular recovery program. Mr. Roosevelt, in his campaign talks, had stressed the importance of expanded purchasing power as necessary for recovery; public works were advocated as a means of stimulating purchasing power and industrial activity; increased agricultural purchasing power through improvement of farm prices was held to be indispensable for general economic recovery.[5] Governor Roosevelt appeared to favor a reflationary program, although no direct support was indicated for a monetary inflation policy.[6]

The first efforts of the new administration were devoted to the solution of the banking crisis. The measures taken to deal with the emergency were eminently successful and laid a basis for the positive program to follow. The adoption of the Agricultural Adjustment Act and the National Recovery Act marked the beginning of the administration's effort to secure recovery.

Business activity, after falling in March, 1933, to within reach of the low point of 1932, began to enjoy a revival. The rehabilitation of the banking structure was the chief explanation for this improvement. The business environment contained various recuperative forces ripe for expression. The extremely low level of prices, along with a depleted volume of consumers' stocks, became immediately more propitious with the prospects of monetary inflation. Inflation was in prospect from two sources: (1) by use of the powers granted to the President under the Emergency Banking Act and (2) in the outlook for increased production costs under the anticipated National Recovery Act.

The expectation of shorter working hours, higher wage rates, and the establishment of codes of fair competition produced a sharp increase in industrial activity in an effort to "beat the codes." It was

[5] "We need to give to 50 million people who depend directly or indirectly upon agriculture, a price for their products in excess of the cost of production. That will give them the buying power to start your mills and mines to work to supply needs. They cannot buy your goods because they cannot get a fair price for their products. . . . A restored agriculture . . . will provide a market for your products. That is the key to national restoration." Governor Roosevelt's campaign speech at Boston.

[6] The Democratic platform here would appear ambiguous in its promise of "sound and adequate currency."

quite apparent that the administration planned to effect some degree of controlled inflation as a business stimulant. This belief was verified by the President's abandonment of the London Conference.[7] The BLS wholesale price index rose from 60 in April to 70 in July, while industrial production jumped sharply from 54 in March to 86 in July, one of the most aggressive advances ever registered.[8]

Such a boom, based upon expected cost and price advances, has its own inherent limitations. Once the anticipated rise had materialized the incentive to further activity was largely dissipated. The course of improvement was not self-reinforcing, since the spurt in production was responsible for heavy inventories, which permitted—or rather, enforced—a curtailment of productive effort.[9] So general was the anticipation of the NRA codes that industrial production reached its high mark in July, 1933, before the codes had become generally effective, and proceeded to decline immediately thereafter.

Just as the NRA was the prime mover in the brief improvement from March through July, it must be debited with the responsibility for the downturn which followed from August through November. This decline was almost as sharp as the preceding rise. The readjustment of the excessive volume of inventories was realized by November, 1933. We have in the NRA boom and collapse, all within a nine-month period, business activity influenced almost entirely by national economic policy.

The failure of the NRA program to inaugurate a recovery prompted a shift in economic policy in favor of emergency public spending. While a very large volume of public works appropriations had been authorized under title II of the NIRA organizing the Public Works Administration, only a small sum was actually expended during 1933.[10] The Federal Emergency Relief Administration, which got under way in the summer of 1933, was designed as the chief vehicle for meeting the broad relief problem. The hasty improvisation of work relief projects under state and local direction proved unsatisfactory, however, and it was soon decided to adopt a federally controlled program. However, the Civil Works Administration, successor to the FERA, was much more than a work relief program; it was

[7] G. Griffith Johnson, Jr., *The Treasury and Monetary Policy, 1933–1938*, pp. 19–20.
[8] The above revised Federal Reserve Board Index of Industrial Production substantially reduces the increase shown in the earlier index.
[9] See the Brookings Institution study of the *National Recovery Administration*, pp. 797–798.
[10] Approximately $110 million.

the administration's first attempt to pursue recovery by a large-scale emergency public works program.

The expansion in public works was designed as a short-run program capable of tiding a portion of the unemployed over the winter of 1933–1934. The consequent stimulus to secondary employment via consumption repercussions was emphasized. The CWA program was highly successful in its objective of immediate expansion as witnessed by the following statistics of monthly outlays.

	Millions		*Millions*
November, 1933	$ 32.0	March, 1934	$124.0
December, 1933	183.0	April, 1934	6.0
January, 1934	219.0	May, 1934	0.1
February, 1934	155.0	Total (Nov. 1933–May 1934)	$719.1

Largely under the influence of the new CWA expenditures, adjusted federal expenditures, as measured by the Krost-Currie series,[11] rose from $300 million for the months of July and August to a peak of nearly $570 million in January, 1934. This rise of almost 100 percent in the adjusted figure was accompanied by a jump in net expenditures in the same period of from less than $100 million to some $320 million—a three-fold rise. The sharp increase produced by the CWA program brought federal outlays to a substantially higher level than had obtained since the close of the period of World War I finance.

Charts IV and V presenting the "Net Contribution" series and the Federal Reserve Board Index of Industrial Production along with the Department of Commerce series of *Monthly Income Payments* and the Department of Agriculture's "Cash Farm Income" series are presented to assist the reader in following the economic fluctuations described in the following pages.

[11] The statistics of expenditures as presented in the *Daily Treasury Statement* are not entirely satisfactory for our purposes. Our interest lies not so much in gross federal expenditures as in those outlays which have a direct bearing upon the level of economic activity. Certain classes of expenditure, such as the transactions of various trust funds, government loans to financial institution to improve their liquidity, and so forth, do not directly affect business conditions. We shall therefore have occasion to use the Krost-Currie series "Net Contribution of the Federal Government to National Buying Power." The gross contribution of the federal government is regarded "as the sum of direct payments made by the Government in the form of income, wages, salaries, interest and rent and other disbursements of the Federal Government which are likely to become income when disbursed by the group to which they are transferred in the first instance." From a mimeographed description of the Net Contribution Series circulated by the Federal Reserve Board. The "Net Contribution" figure is derived by deducting from the gross adjusted expenditures all government receipts deemed to be income-reducing, which includes all receipts except the following: (*a*) estate and gift taxes, (*b*) seigniorage, and (*c*) canal tolls. For a detailed description of the Krost-Currie series see Henry H. Villard, *Deficit Spending and the National Income*, ch. xx, and Appendix I.

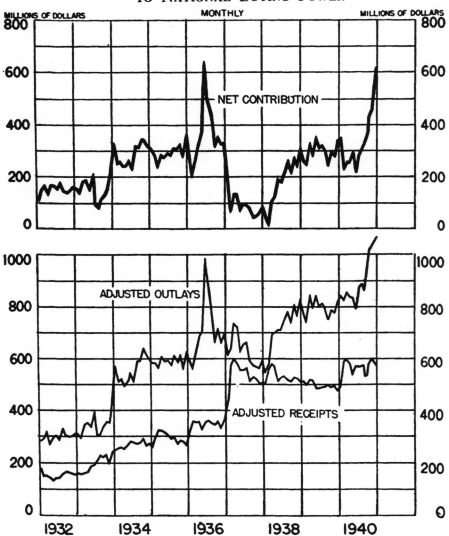

Chart V

The Federal Net Contribution and Economic Activity

FEDERAL NET CONTRIBUTION

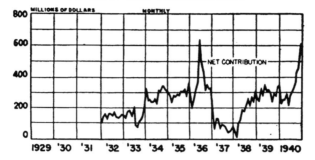

INDUSTRIAL PRODUCTION

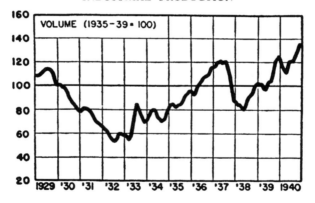

INCOME PAYMENTS AND CASH FARM INCOME

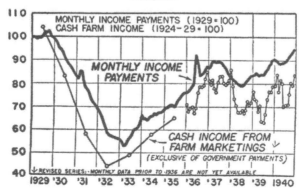

CWA outlays do not appear to have had as beneficial consequences upon business activity as might have reasonably been anticipated.[12] While the upturn in production in the first third of 1934 was probably in part attributable to the CWA, the recovery lasted only briefly and by midsummer of 1934 industrial activity had slumped again to the level prevailing at the bottom of the NRA reaction. The pattern of response realized was quite close to that predicated by the model described earlier on substantially identical premises.[13] But the decline in production during the summer of 1934 occurred in the face of an appreciably higher level of public expenditures than had prevailed in the previous year; for while CWA operations were terminated early in 1934, other classes of expenditures were enlarged.[14]

The rise in federal expenditures, which compensated for the termination of the CWA program and served to maintain federal outlays at a relatively high level, took place in the following categories; (1) FERA appropriations which were expanded greatly upon the closing stages of the CWA program, (2) PWA direct operations as well as grants to states,[15] and (3) Agricultural adjustment aid and farm credit operations.

Viewing the spurt of federal construction activity at the end of 1933 and the beginning of 1934 as a pump-priming effort, it must be judged a poorly conceived attempt, indeed. For it is essential to the success of such a scheme that a retrenchment be postponed until there is some assurance of a continuation of the upward trend. If it were apparent that recovery in industrial production was geared in a measure to the federal construction program (the prominent exception here being automotive production), the consequences of an abrupt termination of that program should have been clear. A pump-priming program cannot by its very nature be tied to a predetermined time schedule, but must, instead, be sufficiently flexible to allow the adjustment demanded by economic developments. Had the construction program been extended, it is conceivable that the recovery might have permitted a curtailment of the program at a later date with no reaction equivalent to that witnessed in mid-1934.

Despite the apparently large size of the public works program, it

[12] See Schumpeter, *Business Cycles*, II, 1002.
[13] That is, a single dose of public expenditures whose effects soon petered out.
[14] The total volume of state and local public expenditures in the fiscal years 1933 and 1934 was practically unchanged.
[15] PWA loans to railroads were substantial during 1934 totaling approximately $140 millions (as measured by cash outlays).

seemed clearly incapable of performing the task set for it. The scope of the CWA program was determined neither by any careful appraisal of the magnitude of the depression problem nor in relation to associated economic measures.

THE MEANING OF WPA

In the summer of 1935 the federal government's approach to spending underwent a substantial reformulation. The chief tangible product of this revised perspective was the creation of the Works Progress Administration as the successor to the FERA program.[16] The federal government was no longer to provide direct relief to the unemployed, but turned this problem over to the states and assumed responsibility for providing work-relief for all employable persons on relief rolls. This new program, which involved the assumption of a heavier and apparently continuing financial burden, was prompted by the realization that despite the moderate degree of economic recovery achieved since 1933, national income still remained at a seriously depressed level, with the volume of unemployment continuing at extremely high figures—an average for January through June, 1935, of about eleven millions.[17] It had become patent by 1935 that full recovery was very far from attainment and that unemployment relief had to be regarded as more than a temporary problem.

Considerations of economy, however, reduced the new WPA program to not much more than a general welfare scheme despite the President's reasoning in his message to Congress that useful public works were an essential ingredient to maintain morale and working ability. "This business of relief must stop" was the declared policy. The rejection of a public works program along PWA lines, capable of stimulating activity in the durable goods area, especially in fields related to the construction industry, was evidence of the administration's desire to reduce the budgetary deficit to a minimum. Whatever stimulus to business was realized from the new relief program would be derived primarily from subsidized consumption, and only to a much smaller extent from government orders for materials, machines, and supplies.

In the subsequent years, through 1940, the WPA and its subsidiary

---

[16] See Williams, *Federal Aid for Relief*, pp. 240 ff.
[17] See chart, "Estimates of Unemployment," appearing monthly in the United States, Social Security Board, *Social Security Bulletin*. We have averaged the series presented for the above period.

programs constituted the major basis of the relief program. The fluctuations in WPA roles were geared closely to variations in the volume of private employment. Any improvement in private employment was soon followed by a downward adjustment in the WPA rolls as conversely a fall in private employment would force an expansion in WPA. The enforcement of the 9 to 1 ratio of reliefers to nonreliefers on WPA rolls, with further limitations of the proportions of funds to be expended on purposes other than wages, assured both the relief character of the program and a minimum schedule of outlay.

The original objective of placing all employables on WPA projects was never realized; the program as operated tended to accept only those individuals in situations of extreme need.[18] WPA rolls expanded quickly after the inauguration of the program in July, and by December of that year about 2,667,000 had been taken on—chiefly transferees from the FERA; operations of the FERA were largely terminated by the end of 1935.

Since under the WPA program the proportion of total funds going for nonlabor purposes, such as purchase of materials, transportation, and so forth, was only 25 percent, the major portion of outlay went indirectly into the purchase of consumers' goods. Because of the condition of the recipients of WPA wages, it is likely that payments to this group were spent more rapidly than the income receipts of any other group in the community. The propensity to consume of this group must be regarded as being in the neighborhood of unity, although undoubtedly some small portion of its wages was used to repay previously accumulated indebtedness.[19]

WPA relief payments were pre-eminently a means of maintaining consumer expenditures at a higher level than would have been possible under the alternative direct relief scheme, although for the group as a whole the standard of living was greatly below that previously enjoyed under private employment.[20] Only under the CWA and PWA programs were wages comparable with earlier incomes. Given the average relief wage, it is to be expected that only the basic necessities

[18] See Senator Burns' preliminary report of the *Special Committee to Investigate Unemployment and Relief, Senate Report No. 1625,* 75th Congress, 3d Session, published April 20, 1938.

[19] This factor need not necessarily reduce their consumption propensity to below unity, since this group as a whole tended to spend more than their wages, such income being supplemented by gifts, various types of subsidies, further loans, and so forth.

[20] It is necessary to point out that while WPA wages were below previous incomes for the group as a whole, for some individuals, especially in the South, WPA wages were greater than earlier earnings.

could be provided with virtually the entire wage being devoted to food, shelter, clothing, and other absolute necessities. Durable consumer purchases, such as refrigerators, automobiles, furniture, sewing machines, and so forth, in the luxury range cannot have received much support from relief expenditures, although it is likely that purchases of second-hand articles of the type listed above were important in the purchases of those on WPA rolls.[21] Minor household durable items, such as radios, electrical goods, house furnishings and equipment, and so forth, may be regarded as within the range of purchases of the above groups.

In general, the WPA program assured the continuity of a certain volume of consumer purchases; it operated, as was true to a lesser degree of the FERA program, to establish a floor to consumer demand. The secondary consequences of any such program upon the durable goods industries and business activity in general is narrowly limited; first, because of the restricted coverage of the plan and second, since such expenditures replaced a previously higher level of consumer demand. The acceleration principle becomes effective only at some point relatively close to full employment.

The public works program operated by the PWA continued to remain an important factor in the activities of the construction industry, although somewhat less significant than in the previous year (1934). The average number of persons employed by the PWA during 1935 amounted to some 330,000 a month, as compared with 476,000 a month in 1934; the total payroll was $308,000,000 in 1934 and $254,-000,000 in 1935. In the entire two and one-half years of the program, from its inception in July, 1933, about $595 million had been distributed in wages, with expenditures for materials on construction projects aggregating approximately $110 million.[22]

PWA construction operations in 1934 and 1935 constituted only a small portion of total construction in these years. The expansion of federal public works activity helped only in small measure to compensate for the much larger drop in private residential, commercial, and industrial construction from an average of almost $6.5 billion in the years 1926–1928 to an average of $1.38 billion for 1932–1934. The PWA cannot be held to have exercised a very substantial compensatory role. When the entire expansion in federal public works appro-

[21] Such dealings in used durable goods of the luxury types can be expected to react favorably upon the market for new products.
[22] *World Economic Review*, 1935, p. 40.

priations for the period is considered, the contrast between the prosperity period and the depression phase is not greatly reduced. The enlarged volume of federal construction activity in 1934 and 1935 failed even to compensate for the decline in state and local appropriations. Considering the post-1929 period as a whole, the movement of federal construction appropriations, when examined in conjunction with state and local activities, cannot be held to have exerted an expansionist stimulus; it served, instead, merely as an antideflationary factor.

TABLE 2 [a]

ESTIMATED EXPENDITURE OF PUBLIC FUNDS FOR NEW PUBLIC CONSTRUCTION,[b] 1930–1940

(Millions of dollars)

Calendar Year	Public Construction Financed by Federal Funds	Public Construction Financed by State and Local Funds	Total Public Construction
1930	307	2,469	2,776
1931	422	2,156	2,578
1932	460	1,334	1,794
1933	647	707	1,345
1934	1,380	794	2,174
1935	1,234	616	1,850
1936	2,335	881	3,216
1937	2,043	845	2,888
1938	2,085	1,103	3,188
1939	2,206	1,314	3,520
1940	2,281 [c]	1,143 [c]	3,424 [c]

a Source: National Resources Planning Board, *Development of Resources and Stabilization of Employment in the U. S.*, Part I (*The Federal Program for National Development*, January, 1941), Table 2, p. 17.
b Including work-relief construction.
c Preliminary estimates.

The general pattern of consumer outlay out of PWA wages probably conformed more closely to previous expenditure habits than did that of the recipients of WPA relief.[23] Consumer outlays, in view of the substantially higher level of income under the PWA, were undoubtedly of a more diversified character than was possible under the relief wage plan. They may be regarded as having been instrumental in maintaining to some degree the market for semiluxury and durable products.

[23] See Williams, *Grants-in-Aid under the Public Works Administration*, chap. v.

Considering 1935 as a whole, the continuation of the high level of public expenditures maintained in 1934 (that is, high in comparison to the volume expended in the years 1931–1933) contributed appreciable support to the consumers' goods industries. Some rough numerical approximation of the importance of federal subsidized consumption may be gained from the fact that all government payments for relief and other special programs totaled in the neighborhood of $2,547 million, which was about 7.8 percent of all retail trade sales in 1935. For 1934 the figure was about 8.4 percent.[24]

The rejection of the PWA pump-priming type of program in favor of the WPA long-range relief-welfare type of spending was not entirely based upon considerations of cost, but was attributable in part to serious doubts that this approach was likely to prove successful. For many members of the administration the failure of the brief CWA program to produce more favorable results soured their enthusiasm for subsequent experimentation. The political considerations raised by the forthcoming elections in 1936 appeared to suggest the wisdom of minimizing the budgetary deficit in the face of the much-voiced business opposition to successive years of badly unbalanced budgets.

DEFICITS AND BUDGETS

The press and business journals had been engaged with remarkable unanimity in attacking the long reign of uninterrupted deficits. While business journals were inclined to admit the short-run stimulative consequences of increased emergency appropriations, they were of a single mind in "viewing with alarm" the long-run effects of a pyramiding of the federal debt structure.[25] The most frequently predicted consequences were (1) the destruction of federal credit leading to a general financial collapse; (2) the realization of a ruinous inflation; (3) a general undermining of business confidence due to fear over the inevitable raising of taxes. The pressure of this sentiment plus the fact that many influential members of the administration entertained similar fears of their own, made the deficits a continuing thorn in the admin-

---

[24] Source: United States Social Security Board, *Social Security Bulletin*, February, 1941, Table 7, p. 65.

[25] See, for example, Kendall K. Hoyt, *The Annalist*, "Business Sectors Likely to Be Benefited by Works Relief Appropriation," XLV (April 19, 1935), 584–585 and "Probable Effect on Business of Beginning of Five Billion Relief Program," XLVI (July 19, 1935), 74 also *The Commercial and Financial Chronicle*, "Looking Backward and Forward at Work Relief," CXLI, Part I (August 24, 1935), 1149–1151, and "Forecasting a Permanent Dole," CXLI (September 21, 1935), 1829–1831.

istration's side. "At least," was their plea, "let us try to reduce our deficits to a minimum."

The administration viewed the successive budgetary deficits with considerable concern. While the increased volume of public appropriations was justified on the score of absolute necessity, the deficits to which they gave rise were viewed with apprehension. This is revealed in the repeated predictions in the first four annual budget messages of the President of the imminent realization of a budgetary balance. There was very little in these early statements to indicate the conversion of the administration to unorthodox fiscal views. The deficits were considered unavoidable, and it was thought that they could and would be corrected in the event of reasonably full economic recovery.

The Roosevelt budget messages justified increased federal appropriations on the ground of their necessity and the contribution they had made to business recovery. "The results of expenditures already made show themselves in concrete form in better prices for farm commodities, in renewed business activity, in increased employment, in reopening of and restored confidence in banks, and in well-organized relief." [26] In referring to the heavy volume of deficits, President Roosevelt said:

This excess of expenditures over revenues amounting to more than $9 billion during two fiscal years has been rendered necessary to bring the country to a sound condition after the unexampled crisis which we encountered last spring (1933). It is a large amount, but the immeasurable benefits justify the cost.[27]

At the same time, however, the President relished a return to a balanced budget. Estimating the total debt at the close of the fiscal year 1935 at $31.8 billion, the President stated that

the Government should seek to hold the total debt within this amount. Furthermore, the Government during the balance of this calendar year should plan to bring its 1936 expenditures, including recovery and relief, within the revenues expected in the fiscal year 1936. . . . We should plan to have a definitely balanced Budget for the third year of recovery (1936) and from that time on see a continuing reduction of the national debt.[28]

In his budget message a year later (January 3, 1935) the President declared that despite the economic recovery realized up to that date, there still remained a substantial volume of unemployment necessitating large relief appropriations.

---

[26] United States, President's Message Transmitting the Budget, Jan. 4, 1934, p. v.
[27] *Ibid.* pp. viii–ix.   [28] *Ibid.*, p. viii.

For this reason it is evident that we have not yet reached a point at which a complete balance can be obtained. I am, however, submitting to the Congress a Budget for the fiscal year 1936 which balances except for expenditures to give work to the unemployed. . . . Such deficit as occurs will be due solely to this cause, and it may be expected to decline as rapidly as private industry is able to re-employ those who are now without work.[29]

The 1936 message (January 3) followed much the same emphasis as had been made in the two previous budget statements. In a somewhat self-congratulatory message attributing the economic recovery to federal fiscal policy, President Roosevelt predicted a balanced budget with the exclusion of relief outlays for 1937. The successive red balances are defended as follows:

Our policy is succeeding. The figures prove it. Secure in the knowledge that steadily decreasing deficits will turn in time into steadily increasing surpluses, and that it is the deficit of today which is making possible the surplus of tomorrow, let us pursue the course that we have mapped.[30]

For further evidence of the success of the administration's economic program, attention was directed to the soundness of government credit which had made possible substantial reductions in the interest payments on government debt obligation.

The Roosevelt administration, whatever else may be said of its spending program, sought to justify the repeated deficits in a manner calculated to minimize public fears over the consequences—in sharp contrast to the alarmist exhortations of the preceding administration.

SUBSIDIZED RECOVERY

The business recovery realized in 1936 was the broadest enjoyed in the economic upturn which had begun in 1933. As in earlier years, federal spending policy must be credited with contributing to the improvement. However, as was true in a lesser degree for 1935, other factors were forging the upturn quite independently of the federal fiscal contribution. While the relief and recovery outlays in 1936 were roughly comparable to those of the previous year, the payment of a huge veterans' bonus in the summer of 1936 raised the federal contribution considerably over the 1935 level. The effect of the bonus payment was particularly marked in consumer purchases during the second half of 1936. The timing of the bonus disbursements during a period of rapid recovery served to accelerate the rate of business ad-

[29] *Ibid.*, 1935, p. x. [30] *Ibid.*, p. vii.

vance beyond the point where it was capable of being long sustained.

Unlike the economic gains of the 1933–1935 period, the advance in 1936 was not restricted to particular areas, but on the contrary was reflected in virtually every sector of the economy. Such lines as construction and durable goods, which had hitherto participated only modestly in the economic improvement, enjoyed in 1936 a substantial measure of recovery. Continued gains were registered in industrial production, farm income, employment and wages, retail sales, corporate earnings, and so forth.[31]

The progress of economic recovery in 1936 was subject to the influence of numerous events, the individual effects of which are difficult to isolate. That year saw the succession of such disrupting developments as the unusually damaging spring floods which hit the Northeast and subsequently the severe drought which visited the entire agricultural area between the Mississippi River and the Rockies. Along with these events were the veterans' bonus payment and the Presidential election campaign. The foreign scene contributed its own quota of disturbing events with the May–June political and industrial crisis in France and the associated monetary distress, developments which finally led to the franc crisis in September and devaluation. The outbreak of the Spanish Civil War in the summer created a situation which threatened to develop into a major European war. The strength of the domestic recovery in the face of these disturbing factors—especially the international developments—is testimony of the vigor of the business improvement.[32]

As mentioned, a significant feature of the progress of recovery during 1936 was the strength of the revival in the durable goods industry. While for the entire year durable goods productions was approximately 20 percent below the 1929 total, for the final quarter of 1936 activity in this area compared closely with that prevailing in the peak year 1929. During the second half of the year the discrepancy existing between the durable and the nondurable class of manufactures which had narrowed during 1935 was largely eliminated, and the relation-

[31] Despite the substantial gains in re-employment, there still remained a very sizable volume of unemployment. Estimates of average unemployment during 1936 vary from nine to eleven and a half million. The lower estimate is Robert R. Nathan's, and the higher is that of the Alexander Hamilton Institute. The growth in the number of employables by more than 4,500,000 between 1929 and 1936 accounts for roughly half the total unemployment figure.
[32] Crum, "Review of the Year 1936," *Review of Economic Statistics*, XIX (February, 1937), 27.

ship which had obtained during 1929 was again approximately realized.

The year 1936 presents a relatively clear example of the short-run consequences of a sharp expansion in the volume of government expenditures. Total expenditures rose from $6.9 billion in 1935 to $8.6 billion in 1936. The most important single development was the prepayment of the veterans' bonus. Other rises occurred in: (1) Regular departments, predominantly by the larger Army and Navy appropriations under the military expansion program; (2) the enlarged relief outlays made by the WPA which by February, 1936, had reached its peak load for the year, with over 3,000,000 persons employed; (3) public works appropriations which reached a new high level. Rental and other payments to farmers fell. With regard to loan operations of government corporations to agriculture and to business, 1936 saw a substantial repayment of outstanding balances. The outstanding volume of government loans to agriculture and business, of which the most important category were RFC loans, was reduced by roughly $600 millions. This heavy flow of funds back to the government was a definite reflection of the business recovery achieved so far.

The veterans' bonus payment on June 15, 1936, in redeemable government bonds and checks, totaled some $1.7 billion. This payment brought total adjusted federal expenditures up from $563 millions in February to almost one billion in June (the procedure adopted by the Krost-Currie series was to average the bonus payments over a six-month period).[33] From June through August adjusted expenditures averaged some $882 millions per month. This level of outlay was considerably in excess of that of earlier periods. The brief spurt in adjusted federal outlays in late 1933 and early 1934 caused by the CWA program was small compared to the stimulus ensuing from the bonus payment. Such an expansion in the government contribution was bound to have a pronounced effect upon the economy. The payment of $1.7 billion to some 3,500,000 veterans was the greatest single stimulus to which the economy had ever been subjected for a comparable period.

Because of the moderate revival in the total volume of expenditures made by state and local governments (which rose from $8,078 million to $8,398 million) [34] and the increase in construction outlays made by

[33] Only half the bonus was included. The expenditure was distributed over the two months prior to the payment, the month of payment and the following three months.
[34] National Industrial Conference Board estimate.

these public bodies, the spending of these governments served to reinforce somewhat the positive influence exerted by the federal government.[35] In previous years, it will be recalled, the persistent reduction in state and local appropriations tended to cancel the stimulating effects attributable to the rise in federal outlays. The WPA program served to lessen the size of the unemployment problem handled by the states and localities. During 1936 the general relief expenditures made by the states declined further because of the upward movement in employment.[36]

Let us examine the consequences of the bonus payment. As will be recalled from our theoretical model on page 17, the effects of a single dose of public expenditures will soon be vitiated unless it succeeds in provoking a certain volume of secondary investment.[37] Given a high propensity to consume, the period retaining the impress of the government stimulus will be longer than that for a lower propensity to consume. While a high propensity to consume might prolong the effects of a single government outlay for many months, no progressive improvement in the level of economic activity is possible without the realization of new private net investment. Such an isolated incident as the payment of the bonus creates a temporary intensive purchasing boom which must be succeeded by a reaction, unless a sufficient volume of new investment has been induced to sustain the new level of consumers' demand.

The June payment of the bonus cannot be viewed as a conscious effort to prime the pump—as was true in the case of CWA and the original formulation of PWA. In fact, the administration forces were opposed to Congressional action on this score, and responsibility for the measure must be attributed to popular clamor for bonus prepayment.

The effects of the bonus payment began to make themselves felt prior to the actual payment.[38] The much-heralded anticipation of the consequences to business of the bonus expenditure gave the business world ample opportunity to prepare for the expected expansion of

---

[35] See Table 2, p. 98.

[36] Total monthly relief payments made by the state governments declined by more than one-third—from $42 millions in January, 1936, to $30 millions in December. In the same period total federal relief payments remained approximately stable. See United States, Social Security Board *Social Security Bulletin*, February, 1941, Chart 2, p. 64.

[37] We are justified in separating the bonus payment from other federal expenditures, since, as will be indicated, this class of outlay had discernibly different characteristics from that of other classes of public expenditures.

[38] See the discussion of Nugent, *Consumer Credit and Economic Stability*, pp. 212–214.

consumer buying. A portion of the rise in inventories during the spring months can be attributed to the prospective expansion of retail trade. The general disposition of business was to view this rise as a purely temporary affair which would subside within a very few months. In retrospect it seems that business failed to appreciate fully the potentialities inherent in the bonus spending.

The character of the stimulus flowing from government subsidized consumer purchases, such as that resulting from the bonus payment, while bearing certain resemblances to the WPA and the PWA type of outlay, is nevertheless quite distinct. The distribution of the bonus without regard for the earning status of the recipient was peculiarly calculated to aid the sales of luxury, semiluxury and all types of durable consumers' goods.

Of the $1.7 billion distributed to veterans, about $1.4 billion was converted into cash before the close of 1936. It appears that about 57 percent or approximately $800 million were expended for consumers' goods and services with the remainder placed in banking accounts, used to pay off consumer credit balances, for business purposes, and so forth.[39] The heaviest portion of the bonus expenditure took place in the months immediately following the distribution of the funds, in June, July, and August; the final four months of 1936 witnessed some further expenditures attributable to the bonus.

The effects of the bonus expenditures were felt in every branch of retail trade, but were particularly evident in the luxury, semiluxury, and durable goods industries. Such items as electric refrigerators, furniture, automobiles, and so forth, were powerfully affected. There is evidence that producers of consumers' goods were none too optimistic over the prospects of any prolongation of such a strong level of demand. In accordance with these sentiments, new capital investment was restricted to the minimum capable of meeting the close-to-capacity levels of operation realized in several fields before the final months of the year. Corporate earnings improved markedly in 1936. As measured by the Standard Statistics index of 161 large corporations, profits rose some 55 percent over 1935 levels and were the highest since 1929, in the final quarter of the year.

While the bonus expenditure was perhaps the chief single stimulus during the year, the developments in the field of consumer credit were well-nigh as important. Measured in dollar terms, the $1,400 million

[39] *Ibid.*, p. 213.

rise in the volume of consumer credit outstanding exceeds the contribution made by the bonus of some $800 actually expended.[40] Nevertheless, a good portion of the growth of consumer credit balances is properly attributable to the installment purchases inspired by bonus checks as well as to the increased level of income and generally more optimistic expectations of consumers. Despite the connection between consumer credit and the bonus payment, this factor does not in the least alter the importance of the great independent stimulus resulting from this quarter. This jump in consumer credit by $1.4 billion was the largest ever recorded for a comparable period and compares with the previous record increase of $1 billion established in 1929.[41]

The continuation of the recovery movement during 1936 must be ascribed predominantly to the stimulus derived from the expansion in consumer purchasing. The rise in income available for new consumers' goods purchases resulting from the bonus payment, plus the huge jump in consumer credit buying, totaled some $2.2 billion; if to this figure there be added the net federal contribution, exclusive of the bonus payment, amounting to $2.4 billion and the unusual Christmas bonuses and dividend disbursements, we reach a total of roughly $5 billion as the "net contribution by consumers" to the national income.[42] Indeed, it is surprising at first glance that the national income in 1936 rose by only $8.8 billion, which would make for a multiplier of less than 2, and jars with our knowledge of a very high rate of expenditures. This low multiplier, however, is explained by the time-lag operative before the impact of the new high level of consumer outlay became fully effective. It was not until the end of 1936 that the various consumer additions were responsible for inaugurating new business investment in producers' and consumers' goods industries. The cumulative strength of the movement appears to have been evident through-

---

[40] This figure is no doubt an understatement of the real volume of expenditures directly attributable to the bonus payment, since in many instances the retention of the bonus check in the bank was a factor making for greater outlays out of current income.

[41] In addition to the above factor, three other factors must be mentioned which, while not of comparable influence, contributed in some measure to enlarge the volume of consumer expenditures. The first was the very large Christmas bonus gifts by numerous business firms to employees; the second was the payment of the largest corporate dividend disbursements ever made; and the third the purchases financed by gains realized and unrealized on the stock exchange. The heavy corporate dividends were largely the by-product of the new tax on undistributed profits. Of the total volume of dividend payments, the greater portion undoubtedly went to individuals with high propensities to save, but it may be hazarded that perhaps some 15-25 percent of the total might have been expended upon consumers' goods. The effects of these additions to consumer purchasing power were concentrated late in 1936 and the immediately following months.

[42] *Ibid.*, pp. 213-216.

out the first two-thirds of 1937, when monthly income payments substantially exceeded the level prevailing during the second half of 1936.

The reluctance of businessmen to undertake new investment in the second half of 1936, because of their sound doubts over the capacity of consumers' demand to be sustained for more than a short time at this high level, was dispelled by the end of the year after the prolonged period of energetic consumer purchasing. It would appear that businessmen revised their earlier skepticism and expressed a disposition, at the end of 1936 and during the first half of 1937, to undertake more freely new investment programs.[43] A multiplier calculated from June, 1936, through June, 1937, would give a far more favorable showing than that based upon 1936 alone.

During the first half of 1937 net business capital formation proceeded at a very rapid rate—at a greater pace, indeed, than that experienced during 1929. For 1937 as a whole, net business capital formation was only slightly below that experienced in 1929.[44] The new investment, as was also true in a lesser degree of the earlier recovery years, was almost exclusively stimulated by consumer expenditures. New investment followed rather than led the higher level of consumer expenditures.[45] No large "independent" volume of net business investment materialized; no emerging industries or innovations provided an outlet for heavy capital investment of the leading type, bringing in its wake enlarged consumer demand. This is the chief distinguishing feature between the economic advance of the twenties and the recovery movement from the depression lows of the early thirties.

THE 1937 RECESSION

The consumer-stimulated recovery enjoyed in 1936 was attended late in that year by the development of various maladjustments which assumed greater importance as 1937 wore on [46] and culminated in an abrupt termination of the long upward swing inaugurated in 1933. The 1937 recession was unusual not alone for the sharpness of the decline but also, more significantly, because of the fact that the downturn took place long before a condition of relative full employment had been realized—contrary to most preceding major economic re-

---

[43] See, for example, the article by La Rue Applegate, "Long-Postponed Additions to Power Plant Capacity Reviving Equipment Sales," *The Annalist*, L. (July 2, 1937), 6–7.
[44] Kuznets, *Commodity Flow and Capital Formation*.
[45] See Hansen, *Full Recovery or Stagnation*, chap. xvii.
[46] See Slichter's article, "The Downturn of 1937," *Review of Economic Statistics*, XX (August, 1938), 97–110.

cessions. The analysis of the factors responsible for precipitating the recession is, therefore, of particular interest to us, since it serves to indicate the limitations of a recovery based largely upon publicly financed consumer expenditures—as opposed to the development of a cycle determined primarily by the "leading" type of business investment.

Before embarking upon an appraisal of the developments responsible for the decline, let us briefly review the major economic series: industrial production achieved its highest level since 1929 in the first two-thirds of 1937. This improvement was restricted to the durable manufactures group, a moderate and persistent decline in the nondurable class taking place throughout the year. While the volume of consumers' goods sales remained relatively constant during the first four months of the year, an improved demand was manifest in the producers' goods industries. New capital investment was proceeding at a pace equal to or greater than that witnessed in 1929.

Total construction activity rose moderately in 1937. Despite the reduction in public construction operations, which took place largely in the federal category, the rise in private building by more than a billion dollars more than offset the curtailment in public activity. The rise in private construction activity was proportionately greater for commercial than for residential construction. In the former class, factory and public utility operations accounted for a good portion of the increase. This improvement in industrial building is explained by the higher levels of economic activity plus the accumulated obsolescence arising from the long hiatus in such construction operations.

Factory employment in 1937 averaged about 8 percent above the preceding year, with the trend continuing upward through September and falling (by about 1,500,000) in the final quarter. The volume of unemployment, however, continued to remain on a plateau throughout the year. As measured by the federal census of unemployment made in November, the number of unemployed was estimated at between 7,800,000 and 10,870,000. As was true of preceding recovery years, the greater improvement was in the durable goods industries. Average hourly earnings in 1937 established a new high mark—some 17 percent above the 1929 level. Average hourly earnings as calculated by the NICB amounted to 69.3 cents, a sharp jump from the 61.7-cent average for 1936. Farm prices, which had begun to rise sharply after June, 1936, because of the drought, continued this increase into 1937, when they reached the highest levels since 1930. After July, 1937, prices declined under the prospective abundant yields. Average farm prices for 1937 were 121 percent of the 1909-1914 base period, as compared with 114 for 1936, 65 for 1932, and 126 for 1930.[47]

Prices of finished and semifinished manufactured goods scored impressive advances in the final months of 1936 and the first quarter of 1937. The Bureau of Labor Statistics index of semimanufactured articles rose from 76.2 in October, 1936 (1929 = 100), to 82.3 in December of that year and then up to 89.5 for April of 1937.[48] This class of prices declined moderately to 85.3 for September, 1937, and then sharply down to 77.7 for December of that year. The prices of finished products as measured by the BLS index rose more moderately and were sustained better in the subsequent recession. Finished products moved up from 82.0 for October, 1936, to 87.4 in April, 1937, and (after a decline had already ensued in the semimanufactured class) further ahead to 89.1 in September, 1937. From this high point a decline to 85.3 was registered for December, 1937. The raw materials commodity class moved less aggressively in the upswing and fell more sharply in the subsequent recession phase. This class rose from 82.1 in October, 1936, to 88.7 in April, 1937, and then after declining moderately to 84.4 in September, 1937, sank swiftly to 75.4 for December, 1937.

Manufacturers' inventories advanced disproportionately to the rate of improvement in industrial production and general economic activity during 1937.[49] While the rise in stocks in the second half of 1936 was associated with an improvement in economic activity, the phenomenal rise in the inventory level, which took place from January through October, 1937, occurred during a period of *stable* industrial production. Inventories expanded out of all proportion to industrial activity. Furthermore, if the volume of production going into inventories is deducted from the total amount of current production, industrial production for current needs was actually declining throughout

[47] Source: United States Department of Agriculture, *The Agricultural Situation*, January 1, 1938, 24.

[48] Slichter notes the growing consumer resistance to higher prices and the serious misjudgment of markets by merchants. "The Downturn of 1937," *Review of Economic Statistics*, XX (August, 1938), 102.

[49] According to the NICB index of manufacturers' inventories (NICB *Economic Record*, December 16, 1939) the volume of inventories rose from 97 in July, 1936, with a slight pause from September through November of that year to 145 in October, 1937. This compares with a level of 130 reached in the spring of 1929 and again in the spring of 1930.

the whole of 1937 [50] from the level reached in the final quarter of 1936.

The explanation of the behavior of manufacturers' stocks is to be found in the commodity price and wage developments in the second half of 1936 and the first half of 1937. As has been described, nonfarm commodity prices and hourly wage rates were experiencing a rapid rise in the above period. The rise of the characteristically sluggish nonfarm and food products price index from 80.1 in October, 1936, to 86.5 in April, 1937, aroused an intensive effort to beat further expected price increases by advance buying. The concomitant rise in hourly wage rates by about 15 percent from September, 1936, to June, 1937, made the race to anticipate further advances still more keen. In addition forward buying was stimulated by fears of interrupted deliveries because of labor troubles. A very important alteration in the direction of consumer credit financing occurred in the middle of 1937—a development which added to the vulnerability of the economic situation.

The rise in consumer credit during the first third of 1937 (when it appears that consumer credit was expanding at a rate of about $145 million a month) [51] acted as a strong supporting factor in sustaining the volume of consumer purchasing power. The contribution of consumer financing declined after April, although it still remained important until about July, when a reduction in credit outstanding was inaugurated which continued throughout the remainder of the year. Nugent explains this reversal in the direction of consumer credit financing by the fact that "by the spring of 1937 . . . households were again well stocked with durable goods and the liberalization of terms was approaching its practical limits. Thereafter expansion of consumer credit was almost entirely dependent upon the further expansion of incomes." [52]

The immediate factor setting off the recession was the sharp drop in the value of new orders making it all too clear that the existing size of inventories was untenable. The decline in raw materials and security prices brought the situation to a head. The failure of a better demand for producers' and consumers' goods to develop in the summer months created an atmosphere of nervousness. With the dissipation of the inflation threat, speculative commodity buying disap-

---

[50] According to Kuznets in *Commodity Flow and Capital Formation*, of the total volume of capital formation for business use in 1937 amounting to $12,720 millions, some $3,337 million or over 26 percent represents net flow to inventories.
[51] Nugent, *Consumer Credit and Economic Stability*, p. 215.   [52] *Ibid.*, p. 217.

peared and inventories were seen to be grossly excessive. To liquidate the inventory accumulation, industrial production was drastically reduced—from an adjusted index (FRB) of 120 in August to 87 in December—one of the most rapid declines on record for a comparable period. Due to the severity of the decline in industrial production, stocks were reduced with a rapidity almost comparable to the speed with which they had been accumulated. By July, 1938, inventories had been restored to the level obtaining at the beginning of 1937 (that is, 113; 1936 = 100).

The alteration in the level of the federal contribution to the economy was a major element in shaping developments in the fall of 1937. The year 1937 was marked by a pronounced drop in federal net expenditures. Federal net expenditures which in 1936 had totaled $4,338 billion, due in part to the bonus payment, fell to $1,114 million in 1937. This latter volume of net income-creating expenditures was the lowest since 1930. After the first month in 1937 the federal net contribution continued on a relatively stable keel at about $100 million a month—as compared with a monthly average of $365 million for 1936. The drop in total adjusted expenditures from $8,568 million to $7,619 million, although substantial, was much less severe than that described by the change in net outlays. Adjusted monthly expenditures which had averaged $600 million in the first quarter of 1936, rose to an average of $784 million for the second and third quarters under the influence of the bonus outlays. In the final quarter adjusted federal expenditures declined to an average of $690 million. Adjusted outlays declined slightly during the first half of 1937 from the level obtaining in the final quarter of 1936. In the second half of 1937 adjusted expenditures dropped farther for an average of $595 million monthly. This moderate reduction in outlays, which represented a fall of one-third from the second half of 1936, was the result of the curtailment of WPA rolls.[53] This cutting of the WPA force was undertaken in response to the increasing volume of employment. According to WPA statistics, however, the reduction in WPA rolls enforced was greater than that justified by the rate of improvement in employment.

Because of the conflicting versions of the role of federal income-

[53] WPA rolls, which had reached a high mark of almost 3 million for the first quarter of 1936, were reduced in subsequent months but raised again in the fall months of 1936. Beginning with December, 1936, WPA rolls were curtailed moderately through May,

stimulating expenditures in the 1937 recession as measured (1) by *total adjusted expenditures*, which declined about 11 percent, or by (2) the volume of *net expenditures*, which dropped by almost 75 percent, it is essential that we determine which figure more accurately reveals the true significance of the altered rate of federal spending.

The highly different pictures of the influence of federal expenditures provided by the two alternative measures of the "federal contribution" are explained by the sharp increase in federal tax receipts. As indicated in our reference to the Krost-Currie series,[54] all federal receipts, with the exception of estate taxes, are treated as deductions from the volume of adjusted expenditures to produce the net contribution figure. The responsibility of increased receipts in bringing about the sharp drop in net expenditures for the year 1937 is indicated in Table 3.

TABLE 3

FEDERAL EXPENDITURES AND RECEIPTS, CALENDAR YEARS 1936–1937

(In millions)

	1936	1937	Difference
Total adjusted expenditures	$8,568	$7,619	$ –949
Total adjusted receipts	4,202	6,505	2,303
Income tax	1,577	2,553	976
Social security taxes	307	1,387	1,080
Internal revenue	1,904	1,918	14
Customs	414	646	232
Net expenditures	4,338	1,114	–3,224

1937, after which date a sharp reduction in WPA employment was effected. The changes in WPA employment during 1936 and 1937 are revealed below.

Month	1936	(In thousands)	1937
Jan.	2,880		2,127
Feb.	3,019		2,145
Mar.	2,960		2,125
Apr.	2,626		2,075
May	2,397		2,018
June	2,286		1,874
July	2,245		1,628
Aug.	2,332		1,509
Sept.	2,449		1,454
Oct.	2,548		1,460
Nov.	2,546		1,501
Dec.	2,243		1,594

Source: *Works Progress Administration*, Report on Progress of the WPA Program, June 30, 1938, page 33.

[54] See page 91n.

PUBLIC SPENDING, 1933–1940   113

We have now to inquire whether or not the above increases in federal receipts did in fact constitute deductions from income which would otherwise have been expended in larger consumer outlays. While the simplifying advantages of the Krost-Currie treatment of receipts are appreciated, the assumption of 100 percent income-reducing tax receipts becomes potentially misleading in the event of a substantial change in the volume of receipts. That is, as long as the relative quantitative relationship existing between receipts and expenditures remains substantially unchanged, the calculation of the net contribution constitutes a comparatively reliable index. But when the volume of receipts changes (as in the above case), the treatment of receipts loses its neutral character and may cause serious misrepresentation of the net contribution figure. We are, therefore, obliged to examine to what extent the additional tax receipts were income decreasing.

We shall restrict our attention to the two chief items of revenue increases: (1) income taxes and (2) Social Security taxes. Internal revenue and customs receipts are held to be income decreasing and do not pose any problems. We shall assume that roughly 75 percent of income tax receipts rest upon savings [55] and that only 25 percent of the increase in personal income tax receipts may be viewed as a deduction against adjusted federal expenditures.[56] With regard to the Social Security taxes, we estimate that perhaps some 50 percent of total levies on payrolls and wages was absorbed by the employer in 1937. All things being equal, one would expect that complete shifting of the tax on employers would be achieved. In fact, however, the shifting of the employers' burden was probably only imperfectly achieved, since, among other things, the development of the recession with its associated price decline made it impossible in many cases for the employer to transfer his burden. As a rough approximation, we estimate that roughly half of the Social Security taxes bearing directly upon the employer may be held as nondeductible from adjusted expenditures. Adding the increase in revenue from the above two classes of tax receipts, we have some $900 million which may be held to be

[55] See United States, National Resources Committee, *Consumer Expenditures in United States*, and United States, Temporary National Economic Committee, *Monograph No. 3*, "Who Pays the Taxes," by Colm and Tarasov, Part III. The above assumption represents no more than a rough approximation.

[56] The fact that income taxes for the calendar year 1937 were collected largely in 1938, a year of relatively poor economic activity, may have decreased the portion of payment which would have been saved.

nonincome decreasing; this figure amounts to almost 40 percent of the addition in tax receipts realized over the 1936 level.

The reduction in the net federal contribution below 1936 on the above basis is, therefore, some $2.3 billion ($2 billion as compared with the 1936 figure of $4.3 billion). While this revised net contribution for 1937 reduces the severity of the drop in federal outlays, it still remains a factor of major importance in shaping the 1937 recession. The inauguration of the regressive Social Security tax program during a period of declining economic activity was a powerful deflationary force which aided the downturn then in progress. The impounding of more than a billion dollars of purchasing power during 1937 diverted this sum away from an industrial establishment sensitively attuned to consumer demand. Had, instead, the 1937 burden of tax collections fallen in the previous year, the consequences of the new tax measures might have proved genuinely beneficial, since they would have served to dampen the speed of the economic advance— thereby possibly prolonging its life span.

Let us venture a brief summary appraisal of the factors responsible for the recession. First it must be recognized that the upturn in progress during 1936 was nurtured primarily by the enlarged volume of federal net-income-creating expenditures. Of almost as great importance in explaining the revival of consumer purchasing power was the growth in the volume of consumer credit outstanding. This consumer-fed recovery had one of its supports removed as a result of the sharp curtailment of federal expenditures in 1937, and another because of the reversal of the upward direction in consumer credit financing in the middle of the year. These developments, timed as they were, were sufficient in themselves to precipitate a recession—one, however, in all probability quite unlike the drastic decline experienced.

The other elements behind the recession, and those responsible for giving the downturn its particular shape, were those relating to the various price and cost changes. The coincidence of appreciable increases in prices of raw materials and labor costs in 1936 and early 1937, sent the prices of semifinished and manufactured products strongly upward. Anticipation of further increases combined with other inflationary considerations brought about a top-heavy inventory pyramid. Excluding the changes transpiring with respect to the level of consumer demand, the above described price and cost phenomena and the associated inventory boom might have been counted upon to burst in some such fashion as it did. There were, of course, other factors which helped to shape the particular course of events in the fall of 1937, but the major elements have been mentioned.

What particular role did the change in federal expenditures play in the 1937 recession? Of equal importance is the question as to what counterinfluence could have been exerted by federal expenditures to avert the recession?

The answer to both questions is really the same. It is primarily a problem of the proper timing of federal outlays in relation to changes taking place in the level of business activity. The very bad timing of the bonus payment in the middle of 1936 served to accelerate the already rapid pace of business recovery to a rate which could be maintained only by a great volume of new private capital investment or by repeated federal expenditures of sums comparable to the bonus payment. While there were indications of the operation of the acceleration principle in the second half of 1936 and the first half of 1937, the process was not proceeding on a self-supporting basis. The coincidence of the collapse of the inventory boom with the fall in the federal government's contribution explained the unusual severity of the 1937 recession. The bad timing of the introduction of the Social Security taxes served to reinforce rather than to combat the downturn. In an immediate sense, the reduction in federal outlay was a contributory rather than a prime cause of the recession. However, since the broad advance inaugurated in 1936 was largely attributable to government-subsidized consumption, the reduced stimulus from this source during 1937 must be judged as perhaps the principal explanation for the subsequent downturn.

The above analysis, it should be clear, has proceeded entirely on the short-term level. It would be entirely unwarranted to deduce from the 1937 episode an argument against reducing the federal contribution at any point short of full employment or the inference that compensatory fiscal policy is the sole solution to the problem of idle resources. Rather, the conclusion may well be drawn that the above experience has demonstrated the deficiencies inherent in compensatory spending as a monistic cure. This issue will be discussed in some detail in the following chapter.

POLICY, SPENDING AND RESULTS

The alarm of the Roosevelt administration over the turn of events in the fall of 1937 was quickly evident in the reversal of the existing monetary policy from one of restriction to one of expansion. In 1936 and the first months of 1937 federal monetary policy discouraged inflation. No doubt there existed some potential inflationary dangers from the credit side, although business conditions remained at a level well below 1928 and 1929. Despite the incomplete nature of the business recovery in 1936 and 1937, demand deposits in member banks in 1936 were much higher than in 1929. The new high accumulation of gold with pyramiding reserves gave tremendous scope to the possible credit expansion. To reduce the inflationary possibilities inherent in such a situation, member bank reserve requirements were raised and the Treasury sterilized further gold acquisitions in an inactive account.

The reversal in the administration's monetary policy followed quickly on the turn in business. Beginning late in August, 1937, the reserve banks reduced their discount rates and the Treasury sought to further ease the credit situation by releasing $300 million of gold from the inactive account in mid-September. The rules governing the eligibility of commercial paper for rediscount at the reserve banks were liberalized. In November margin requirements were reduced and open market operations (on a small scale) were undertaken by the Federal Reserve banks. The Treasury followed up its "limited sterilization program," announced in February, 1938, with the desterilization of the $1.4 billion of gold accumulated since December, 1936.[57]

While the administration's "easy" monetary policy served appreciably to counteract the progress of monetary and economic deflation, the spending and lending program advocated by the President in April, 1938, and approved by Congress in June constituted the main burden of the attack on the recession. However, the long lapse between the beginning of the business slump in the late summer and fall of 1937 and the proposal of a new relief and recovery program in April, 1938 (a delay of some eight or nine months during a period of sustained business recession), indicated the reluctance of the administration to resort to such measures. The recession in 1937, precipitating a keen struggle between the budget balancers and the opposing spending factions, each seeking to sway the President's decision, brought into bold relief the long inner conflict which had characterized the Roosevelt administration's fiscal and budgetary philosophy.

[57] Gold certificates were deposited in the Federal Reserve banks against the gold held by the Treasury. Banking reserves are increased as the Treasury pays out funds in meeting its obligations and the funds move into the commercial banks.

The split personality of the administration with respect not only to spending policy but economic policy in general (as between the conservative and liberal factions) emphasized what had been clear since 1933—the absence of a consistent economic philosophy. During the months after the recession got under way the economy-minded group, with Secretary of the Treasury Morgenthau as their representative, were in the saddle. It was not until the spring of 1938 that the President shifted his alliance to the camp of the spenders.

Secretary Morgenthau voiced the position of the economy group in a speech before the Academy of Political Science on November 10, 1937.[58] The temporary eclipse of the "spending" advocates was shown by the Secretary's rejection of arguments favoring a renewed spending drive and his advocacy of the need for a balanced budget. The Secretary stated:

The basic need today is to foster the full application of the driving force of private capital. We want to see capital go into the productive channels of private industry. We want to see private business expand. We believe that much of the remaining unemployment will disappear as private capital funds are increasingly employed in productive enterprises. We believe that one of the most important ways of achieving these ends at this time is to continue progress toward a balance of the federal budget.

Dismissing the idea of attaining a budgetary balance by increasing the tax load, Mr. Morgenthau proposed that it be achieved by reducing federal expenditures in the following fields: (1) public highways; (2) public works other than highways; (3) unemployment relief; and (4) agricultural benefits. By reducing expenditures in the above categories by some $700 millions, the net deficit estimated by the President in his budget summary of October 19, 1937, for the fiscal year 1938 could be wiped out. Mr. Morgenthau cautioned against a too-drastic reduction in expenditures, but said: "I strongly favor a vigorous program for the progressive reduction of federal expenditures to the minimum demanded by the government's responsibilities."

While an additional $250 millions was appropriated early in March to provide for the expanded relief requirements, no reversal in the economy approach expressed above was clear until President Roosevelt, on April 12, 1938, in a special message to Congress, asked for the adoption of a "spend-lend" program totaling $4.5 billion. In his message the President, attributing the 1937 recession to a deficiency of

[58] "Federal Spending and the Federal Budget," *Proceedings of Academy of Political Science*, XVII, No. 4 (January, 1938), 534–542.

consumer purchasing power, took the position that only a vigorous increase of public expenditures would insure a prompt economic recovery. In the above address Mr. Roosevelt gave expression to a budgetary doctrine more unorthodox than any of his previous statements on fiscal policy. The general viewpoint expressed was that which had been associated with Mr. Eccles [59] of the Federal Reserve Board and the liberal New Deal spending group; in its more aggressive form it has come to be known as "compensatory spending policy." This theory, as earlier described, accepts deficit financing as a necessary means for achieving a high level of national income in the absence of an adequate volume of private investment. Endorsement of this position, however, implies no set course of budgetary policy, but merely expresses the conviction that apprehension with regard to deficits should not be the determining consideration in the formation of the budget.

Carried out in full measure, compensatory spending calls for the substitution of public investment for deficiencies in private investment to the point at which relatively full employment has been achieved. To realize this goal in 1938 would have necessitated a spending and lending program aggregating roughly $10 to $15 billion. Such an audacious program, however, appeared politically inexpedient, and the proposed relief and recovery outlays were much lower. While many of the following excerpts from the President's message bear resemblance to earlier arguments for enlarged public outlays, the absence of any immediate consideration for near-term achievement of a balanced budget marks this expression as belonging to a new genre of fiscal faith—although the proposed spending program could very well have been advocated on the basis of emergency needs, as in the past.

President Roosevelt, in his April 12 message, submitted that the 1937 recession, like the 1929 decline, arose from deficiency in consumer purchasing power. "In other words, production in many important lines of goods outran the ability of the public to purchase them." The deficiency of consumer demand must be rectified.

Today's purchasing power—the citizen's income of today—is not sufficient to drive the economic system at higher speed. Responsibility of Government requires us at this time to supplement the normal processes and in

---

[59] The public papers of Mr. Eccles have been edited by Rudolph L. Weissman and have been published under the title *Economic Balance and a Balanced Budget*.

so supplementing them to make sure that the addition is adequate. We must start again on a long steady upward incline in national income.

National income . . . is now running at the rate of about fifty-six billions. If it can be increased to $80,000,000,000 in the course of the next year or two, the whole economic picture will be different. Hundreds of thousands more people will be employed in private industry, hundreds of thousands fewer will be in need of relief, and consumer demand for goods will be greatly stimulated.

Let us unanimously recognize the fact that the Federal debt, whether it be twenty-five billions or forty billions can only be paid if the Nation obtains a vastly increased citizen income. I repeat that if this citizen income can be raised to $80,000,000,000 a year the National Government and the overwhelming majority of State and local governments will be "out of the red." The higher the national income goes the faster will we be able to reduce the total of Federal and State and local debts.

The above ideas, although given a somewhat new expression, are quite close to the earlier notion of pump-priming advanced as early as 1933. Indeed the resemblances to the pump-priming theory would seem to be greater than to the compensatory spending theory. As expressed in the *size* of the program, the theory, or rationalization, appears not far away from the earlier pump-priming thesis.

In addition to the above proposed program, Congress authorized expenditures of some $750 millions, bringing the total emergency appropriations to $5,250,000,000. Of this sum, $1,400 million was to be financed by the proceeds of desterilized gold, $500 million to be taken from the working balance in the general fund and approximately $680 millions to be derived from social security and other trust funds with the remainder to be borrowed in the open market.

It was recognized that the success of the emergency spending program depended upon the speed with which it could be inaugurated. To this end everything was done to hasten the operation of the authorized program. But while the relief portion of the program was capable of rapid acceleration, the public works projects proved again to be difficult to get under way in less than four to six months. The rise in adjusted federal expenditures in the first half of 1938 was largely the product of the expanded WPA program. Public works expenditures were lower in this period than for the comparable period in 1937. The volume of RFC loans failed to expand in the manner that had been expected—the total of loans made in the first half of 1938 amounting to $189 million as compared with $200 million in the second half of 1937 and $273 million for the second half of 1938.

Under the emergency program WPA employment rose appreciably, from an average of about 1,500,000 persons in the final third of 1937 to an average of 2,165,000 in the first third of 1938, moving up steadily to more than 3,150,000 persons for the final four months in 1938. Monthly WPA expenditures for wages rose from an average of about $83 million a month in the last four months of 1937 to $112 million in the first four months of 1938, $150 million for the second third, and an average of $169 million for the final third. Regular public works outlays, which had totaled some $375 million in the first half of 1938, rose to $540 million for the second half of that year. The $300 million expended in the final quarter of 1938 established a new high level of regular federal construction outlays.

From all indications, business expectation of the consequences of the 1938 emergency spending program appears to have been the dominant factor in inaugurating the rapid upsurge of activity in the durable manufactures industries beginning in June of that year. Certainly on the basis of the current state of consumer demand and the comparatively high level of manufacturers' inventories, no such sharp resurgence of productive activity appeared justifiable—especially given the continuing downward movement of wholesale prices and the threatening international situation. The behavior of stock market prices seems to confirm this opinion. For it was not until April, 1938, simultaneously with the announcement of the gold desterilization program, the reduction of reserve requirements and the Presidential proposal of the large emergency spending program, that the protracted decline in security prices, inaugurated in August, 1937, was arrested. While the business journals reiterated their dire predictions of the ultimate disastrous consequences of deficit-financing fiscal policy, they were equally unanimous in admitting that in the short run such a program was bound to have stimulative consequences. This conviction appears to have derived considerable strength from the still fresh recollections of the powerful repercussions of the federal expenditures of 1936. Indeed, it appears that not a few businessmen had been converted to expansionist public spending and were strongly advocating such measures after the 1937 recession.[60]

[60] These converts were, nevertheless, clearly in the minority and were more usually small retailers than big industrialists. The popular press and the business journals appear

The improvement in business activity in the second half of 1938 must be attributed almost entirely to the various measures, both monetary and fiscal, adopted by the federal administration. Considered by itself, this legislation represents the most successful attempt by the New Deal to influence the course of business developments. The only comparable effort was the CWA spending program in the winter of 1933–1934—which was only half-way successful, because of the economic decline shortly after the termination of the program. Unlike the CWA and the unwanted bonus payment episode in 1936 (unwanted by the administration) the 1938 relief and recovery program was not a concentrated splurge of spending, but rather a comparatively rapid-starting program, which reached its peak within approximately nine months and then slowly tapered off. While the public works portion of the program suffered from unnecessary delays, the quick expansion of relief payments served to reduce the consequences of this deficiency. A major criticism that can be levied against the program is the rather considerable delay between its inauguration and the development of the recession during 1937. But this was primarily a reflection of the indisposition of the administration to accumulate any larger deficit than was absolutely imperative.

In 1939 the administration pursued its past policy of reducing WPA employment at a much faster rate than that justified by the pace of improvement in private employment. Although caring for only approximately 25 percent of the total number of unemployed late in 1938, work relief was rapidly reduced, despite relatively stable levels in both employment and payrolls; these latter two series did not begin to move upward until the second half of the year.

While the federal contribution continued to be an important factor during the final third of 1939, along with the favorable level of construction operations, the economic repercussions following swiftly in the wake of the declaration of war were the dominant influences responsible for the sharp business advance in this period. Apprehension over the longer-term consequences liable to stem from a Euro-

to have been successful in marshaling business opinion strongly against expansionary fiscal policy.

It was estimated that newspaper editorials were opposed to the President's 1938 program by a ratio of six to one. McConnell, "The Press Looks at Pump Priming," *Current History*, XLVIII (June, 1938), 30–32. The Gallup poll (April, 1938) and *Fortune* poll (March, 1939) registered majority opposition to government spending in general. However, support was elicited for specific items.

pean war was submerged in the immediately heightened prospects for industries likely to benefit from large-scale war orders.

RECOVERY POLICY TAKES A BACK SEAT

The year 1939 thus marks the first period since the inauguration of the recovery moment in 1938 in which federal expenditures relinquished their place as the chief factor in the economic situation. For while such outlays continued to be of great importance throughout 1939, the declaration of war in September made this new factor the dominant element in the economic picture. Measured by the actual volume of foreign war-purchasing in 1939, the initial importance of this event was grossly over-rated; nevertheless, the psychological expectations stimulated by the outbreak of war were largely responsible for shaping the pattern of economic developments in the final four months of the year. Furthermore, with the advent of the European war and the growing German threat, American armaments expenditures were bound to jump skyward with the consequent reorientation of the economy to huge domestic military purchases. While the United States defense appropriations had been steadily on the upgrade since 1934, the period following the opening of actual hostilities and the subsequent Hitler victories was marked by a tremendous expansion of such outlays, making the successive defense programs the prime determining factors in the economic situation.

TABLE 4

NATIONAL DEFENSE EXPENDITURES [a]

(In millions of dollars)

		1940 (Monthly)				1941 (Monthly)		
1934	$ 531	Jan.	$132	July	$177	Jan.	$569	July	$ 960
1935	689	Feb.	129	Aug.	200	Feb.	584	Aug.	1,124
1936	900	Mar.	143	Sept.	219	Mar.	748	Sept.	1,320
1937	929	April	159	Oct.	287	April	763	Oct.	1,527
1938	1,029	May	154	Nov.	376	May	837	Nov.	1,437
1939	1,206	June	153	Dec.	473	June	812		
1940	1,657								

[a] Source: Bulletin of the United States Treasury Department.

The course of events in 1940, after the reaction in the first quarter to the speculative inventory accumulation inherited from 1939, was largely determined by the developments in the European war. The export demand for war materials was joined by the inauguration of an enormous national defense program prompted by the astonishing German victories in the Lowlands and France in the spring of 1940. The sudden realization of the military strength of the Nazis and the consequent revaluation of the scope of our defense requirements found expression in a domestic armaments program of unprecedented peacetime magnitude. Under the twofold stimulus of enlarged foreign war orders plus the growing national defense effort, national income produced rose to $73.9 billion, which, when adjusted for the difference in prices between 1929 and 1940, meant that in terms of physical output the 1929 totals were surpassed by a considerable margin.

Defense expenditures and subsequent war outlays are, in a sense, carrying to fruition the expansionist spending doctrines expressed during the 1930's. The enormous war-spending program is achieving what peacetime relief and recovery outlays failed to accomplish. Our analysis of the details of the successive Roosevelt spending programs has only incidentally touched upon the broader issues relating to the determination of the scope and limitations inherent in spending policy. The following chapter, accordingly, is devoted to this topic.

VII. THE LESSONS OF NEW DEAL SPENDING

RESULTS

THE EXPERIENCE of the Roosevelt administration with fiscal policy cannot be judged to have been very successful. While relief and recovery outlays did absorb some idle resources and contributed, through secondary effects, to a higher level of economic activity, the hoped-for results failed to materialize. Throughout the decade we were plagued with enormous unutilized productive facilities. The average unemployment figure for the years 1933–1940 was in the neighborhood of ten million, with a low of approximately eight million. The limited gains attributable to deficit spending have been submitted as evidence of the bankruptcy of this policy. Proponents of compensatory fiscal policy, on the other hand, have countered that the specific Roosevelt spending measures have been at fault and have done a great disservice to the general policies advocated. In the present chapter we shall attempt to establish the potential scope of compensatory fiscal policy as revealed by the experience of the thirties.

As indicated in the preceding chapter, the successive spending measures of the Roosevelt administration were primarily short-run emergency expedients—relatively far removed from any consistent application of some variant of public spending doctrine. In effect, the various spending programs were dominated by considerations pertaining to relief rather than to recovery. The relief aspect is apparent in the minimization of all nonwage payments in every program with the exception of PWA and, in a limited degree the CWA. The ultimate decision in 1935 to administer a work relief program of the WPA type was contrary to the original, more ambitious, objective envisaging a genuine public works program. Equally significant was the fact that the federal government failed to admit more than a fraction of the unemployed population to the WPA payroll—contrary to its stated policy of providing employment for all the employable unemployed. The spending activities of the administration were conservatively conceived, despite the large costs involved. Sensitive to accusations of financial profligacy, the Roosevelt administration sought to minimize budgetary deficits. The disparity between the later vigorous fiscal enunciations emanating from the White House and the actual programs adopted has been marked.

The recovery and relief objectives have never been clarified. Evidences of the shifting goals and uncertain policies were manifest throughout the years 1933–1940 by the succession of rapidly changing programs. Reversals of position have revealed the uncertainty surrounding the measures adopted. The conflicting philosophies of different governmental departments have repeatedly clashed. While the FERA and WPA programs were designed primarily as measures to alleviate human distress, the projects themselves have been supported on grounds of their general stimulative consequences. Fluctuations in spending have been narrowly geared to short-run variations in business activity. The volume of outlays has not been determined by the objective of full employment, but rather by the dictates of social and political necessity.

Relief and recovery expenditures appear to have constituted the most important influence upon the course of economic activity in the years 1936–1939. Federal spending 1933–1935 exercised only minor control, being subordinate to other New Deal measures. With the outbreak of war in September, 1939, the direction and emphasis of public spending underwent a profound change and the war became the dominant factor in the business picture. The Roosevelt monetary program constituted an indispensable adjunct to the various spending measures, making available, as it did, the necessary funds. Up to the fall of 1937 the recovery movement was based in good measure upon federally subsidized consumer purchasing reinforced significantly by a rise in consumer credit. The producers' goods industries, rather than leading the upswing, as had been characteristic of earlier recoveries, followed the improvement of consumer outlays and were gauged closely to this expansion. The upturn succeeding the 1937 recession was largely the product of enlarged federal outlays. No substantial volume of independent business investment materialized throughout the entire decade. The relatively meager results achieved, however, reflect more the restricted scale of spending than any absolute failure of compensatory spending per se.

TAX POLICY AND SPENDING POLICY

Federal tax policy during the period under discussion failed to coincide with the stated objectives of spending policy. The adoption of numerous miscellaneous manufacturers excise and consumption taxes along with the processing and payroll tax served to counteract the reflationary program of the administration. We have noted particularly the adoption of the regressive Social Security levies at the same time increased mass purchasing power was advocated as a means of achieving a higher level of economic activity. The revenue program appears to have been developed entirely independently of the expansionist spending policy.

Donald W. Gilbert, in a very interesting article,[1] has constructed a "Federal Tax Ratio," expressing the changing proportions of total tax receipts derived from taxes bearing upon consumption as compared to those weighing upon savings. Upon the basis of his estimates for the years 1929–1939 he concludes that federal taxation "worked in reverse gear."

When business declined, recession being hastened by the resultant collapse of consumer spending, taxes which further reduced consumer purchasing power bulked relatively large among federal revenues. This swing to spending taxes was due partly to the collapse of the corporate and personal income tax revenues (primarily saving taxes) and partly to the initiation of the new spending taxes on manufacturers and liquor levied as a means of bolstering up the disintegrating federal finances.[2]

The subsequent rise in the yield of corporate and personal income taxes (partly as a result of the rise in rates) served to some extent to correct the earlier development noted above. The sharp decline in the ratio of tax yield from the spending stream relative to savings in the years 1934 and 1938 [3] tends to modify, somewhat, Mr. Gilbert's conclusions. But the "Federal Tax Ratio" realized from consumption in the most favorable years 1936–1938 was considerably above that enjoyed in the late twenties and, in the perspective of the administration's manifest spending objectives, failed to support these latter measures.

Equally important with the quantitative considerations listed above are those relating to the qualitative aspects of the taxes adopted. As

---

[1] "Taxation and Economic Stability," *Quarterly Journal of Economics*, LVI (May, 1942), 406–429.
[2] *Ibid.*, pp. 422–423.   [3] See Chart 1, *ibid.*, p. 420.

earlier noted, the federal tax program weighed onerously upon business investment and, through the neglect of proper credit for capital losses, discouraged speculative capital enterprise.[4] The entire tax program, for that matter, appeared to be designed without any great regard for the burden imposed upon business incentives in general. The mistaken tendency to regard taxable capacity as a corporate rather than a personal capability underlay much of the Treasury's tax proposals. The successive tax measures of the administration formed no coherent pattern, but like the spending program itself appeared to be determined by the exigencies of the moment.

THE VOLUME OF PUBLIC SPENDING

Aside from the above deficiencies, how are we to explain the very limited and short-lived results of New Deal spending measures? The Hansenian school attributes the disappointing results to the restricted scale of compensatory operations [5] and, to a minor extent, to the defective timing. In discussing the scale of public outlays required to realize full employment *The Economist* of London has the following to offer:

This figure (the volume of public expenditures deemed necessary to purchase full employment) is very much larger than is usually realized, and its magnitude serves to illustrate why it is that attempts by Governments have in the past so frequently failed to produce any effect on the state of trade. Mr. Lloyd George's proposals a dozen years ago envisaged the expenditure of £200 millions, and though this was considered to be an impossibly large sum in terms of the public finances, it was obviously too small to exercise any dominant effect on the conjuncture. The American equivalent to the British figure of £1,200 millions (estimated new investment required to secure full employment in 1938) would be something like $20 or $25 billions, and Mr. Roosevelt's peacetime deficits of $4 or $5 billions, for all the shouting they provoked, were obviously not in proportion to the problem. Indeed, the quantitative approach provides a clear illustration of the importance of private investment. When the required total is £1,200 millions, a "public works" program of £200 millions may

[4] See Angell, *Investment and Business Cycles*, chap. xiii.
[5] Burns and Watson, in *Government Spending and Economic Expansion*, p. 106, declare: "Whether we relate the volume of spending to total national income or to that part of it which is investment, the volume of spending must be increased in order for spending to be effective. In the conditions which have prevailed in the 1930's, a little spending—a few hundred million a year—accomplishes little and is highly inconclusive. Spending in moderate amounts—two or three billion a year as in 1934 and 1935—serves to maintain activity or even to increase it slowly but does not bring about recovery. A large volume of deficit spending—upwards of five billion a year—cannot help but bring increased private investment and economic expansion, if spending is continued as long as is necessary."

easily do positive harm, if the circumstances of its announcement are such as to create an atmosphere of alarm and frighten the private individual or institution with money to lay out.[6]

There can be no dispute with the contention that full employment can be secured if federal expenditures are sufficiently expanded. Irrespective of the "multiplier" and the response of private investment to enlarged government outlays, all resources can be employed, given an unlimited public budget—in the event that inflationary pressures can be effectively controlled and the national credit system successfully insulated. The generous predictions of ruinous inflation and financial collapse made during the thirties, in accompaniment to the recurrent budgetary deficits, have served to obscure the real character of the issues involved. The basic problem is not whether public spending can achieve full employment, but whether this method is *superior* to alternative means.

Hansen and those of his faith in effect force the conclusion that compensatory government spending is the sole answer to the problem of idle resources. The revitalization of private enterprise is excluded as an alternative solution, since stagnation is attributed to purely external phenomena (the factors of economic progress), over which man is powerless. This approach constitutes an eloquent argument for restricting positive measures to the public sector of the economy. The salvation of private enterprise is made dependent upon an extension of publicly-sponsored activity rather than the correction of the factors immediately related to idle resources.

IS SPENDING THE CURE?

Resort to the public purse, however necessary and valuable an expedient, cannot be heralded as a cure for the ills giving rise to depressions. Public spending as practiced during the thirties accepted prevailing institutional maladjustments and sought recovery (insofar as federal spending constituted a recovery as opposed to relief effort) [7] through the general subsidization of purchasing power and

---

[6] From an article entitled "Full Employment: the Means," *The Economist*, October 10, 1942.

[7] "It can be said . . . that decreasing reliance was placed upon the effects of public works expenditures in stimulating business recovery, and that in the later years of the period, such expenditures had as their major objective the alleviation of the distress caused by unemployment." United States, National Resources Planning Board, *Development of Resources and Stabilization of Employment in the United States*, January, 1941, p. 17.

encouragement to the heavy goods industries.[8] The large-scale lending activities to distressed home owners, farmers, financial institutions, railroads and business establishments fulfilled the function of immediate salvage, but were unaccompanied by more far-reaching reconstruction measures (with the exception of the various banking reforms). Where prices were abnormally depressed, as in the agricultural field, steps were inaugurated to restore a healthier level. For the price structure as a whole, however, with specific reference to the wide range of administered prices and restrictive trade practices, no satisfactory reconstruction program has been formulated, let alone prosecuted. As will be indicated in the following chapter, the trust-busting efforts of Thurman Arnold and the Anti-Trust Division of the Justice Department have not only failed to achieve any tangible benefits but also have manifested an inability to comprehend the significance of imperfect competition and related market phenomena.

Heavy public construction outlays will not lead to a significant revival in private housing activity if high, inflexible building material prices are left unchanged and if no means is found for reducing hourly wage rates (a development which would be highly advantageous for the building trades). Moreover, the neglect of a more systematic reduction of mortgage costs than that provided by the Home Owners Loan Corporation and the failure to assure a freer flow of mortgage funds to private individuals left unrealized the full scope of potential encouragement to the construction industry available from this quarter. However, as a practical proposition it is, of course, not possible to isolate building materials for special price action. Rather, the effective reduction of building material prices obliges intervention in a very large segment of the durable goods field—a formidable task indeed. With respect to the untenably high building trades wage rates, which have constituted a serious impediment to a private residential construction recovery, agreements between the building trade unions and the government and / or construction corporations guaranteeing annual earnings might be made the basis for establishing a more economical wage structure.

Modification of prevailing price practices, financing methods, and wage rates does not exhaust the avenues through which private residential construction, as an example of specific action, may be encour-

[8] We have noted how small were the proportions of the federal construction program relative to the decline in private construction outlays.

aged. During the thirties American housing construction failed to take advantage of the mass production practices which have proved so successful in Great Britain. Our construction techniques have failed to progress much beyond the level of efficiency realized during the 1920's. Great savings are available if the traditionally small-scale, handicraft type of operation is superseded by the most advanced construction methods available.

The investigations of the Temporary National Economic Committee have provided a vast storehouse of data pertaining to noncompetitive price behavior and restrictive trade practices. The great area of our economy disclosed to be subject to the sway of imperfect competition, privatization of markets, and a wide variety of trade restraints reveals the magnitude of the problem confronting us in any program designed to achieve a more efficiently functioning market. This knowledge has acted to discourage activity in this direction. The preliminary painstaking investigation required to identify and evaluate the infinite variety of restrictive price and trade practices of different industries, the subsequent formulation of remedial policy, and the ultimate expression of the findings on the administrative level pose an array of enormously complicated problems. The dividends, moreover, of such a program are not likely to materialize promptly, but rather become evident only after a considerable period of gestation. The great political and psychological virtue of public spending —whatever be the object of the outlay, resides in the rapidity of the economy's response—given an adequate spending hypodermic. The more fundamental cure, effected by correcting the specific elements contributing to imperfect market performance, is likely to be a relatively slow process compared to an aggressive spending program, which shows results almost immediately. The opposition, moreover, of the business and labor groups, obliged to alter their pricing and trade practices, makes any earnest public effort in this direction a hazardous political enterprise indeed.

THE IDEOLOGY OF SPENDING

One of the serious ideological consequences of a public spending program—as manifest by the experience of the thirties—is the tendency of such programs to distract attention from detailed investigation into specific institutional maladjustments. Public spending, oper-

LESSONS OF NEW DEAL SPENDING 131

ating as it does primarily through a generalized pressure upon the income stream and, in subsidiary measure, upon the heavy goods industry, leads to a preoccupation with the size of the aggregate income flow rather than the nature of the performance of the market for particular sectors of the economy and the problems confronting specific industries. Implicit in the orientation of the compensatory spending school is the belief that the realization of a high income level will automatically rectify prevailing cost-price maladjustments and other manifestations of ill health. The failure of public outlays to achieve the desired results can always be attributed to an inadequate volume of expenditures. In like manner, a downturn such as that of 1937 can be laid to a fall in the government contribution. Nominally, this contention is correct although it may conceal a larger truth.

Another disconcerting aspect of public spending programs—in the United States as well as most foreign countries—is the fact that they represent essentially a domestic type of recovery program. With the government committed to the quest of recovery through expansionist outlays, attention is inevitably focused upon domestic rather than international problems. The President's abandonment of the London Economic Conference of 1933 and the subsequent failure of the United States to assume leadership in the reconstruction of international trade and foreign economic relations signified our preoccupation with domestic problems.[9] The administration retreated into the domestic sphere at the expense of more energetic participation in the solution of international trade and monetary maladjustments. The ultimate costs of this policy must be appraised not alone in terms of the disorganized and depressed international trade of the thirties but also in relation to the culmination of this period in World War II. While the Reciprocal Trade Agreements Policy of the administration represented a very useful departure from the rising wave of discriminatory trade barriers, it cannot be viewed as having exerted any major influence in reorienting the course of world trade during the thirties. In this sphere, too, it would appear that the attraction of immediate gains in the domestic field attendant upon a reflationary monetary and fiscal program were held to outweigh the slower and less spectacular dividends held out by an attack upon the involved problems of international economic reconstruction.

[9] See Johnson, Jr., *The Treasury and Monetary Policy 1933–1938*, pp. 19–20.

The above recommendations, calling for an attack upon (1) restrictive domestic market policies, (2) special industrial problems such as those, for example, confronting the construction, railroad, and bituminous coal industries, and (3) the reconstruction of international trade and economic relations, represent a most ambitious program.[10] It is obviously impossible to predict to what extent such an attempt is likely to succeed. Not only does there exist considerable question as to the precise nature of the desired reforms, but the actual implementation of the conclusions reached presents a most formidable political and administrative task. It would be wishful thinking indeed to assume that the multitude of perplexing problems involved will all be satisfactorily resolved. There will undoubtedly remain a large area wherein only partial success will have been achieved. To the extent that the economy is burdened with unemployed resources —both cyclical and secular—it will be necessary to supplement the program outlined above with an appropriate fiscal program. Moreover, as will be indicated in the succeeding chapter, international governmental loans will probably be called upon to play a vital role in world economic reconstruction. Our domestic fiscal program will have to be integrated with foreign financial operations.

The need for a domestic compensatory spending program in the orientation suggested above is essentially residual, being a function of the relative success realized in the broader reconstruction plan. The attainment of the recovery goals and the maintenance of a high level of income will inevitably depend upon the quality of the diagnosis achieved. A recovery plan addressed to the resolution of more than short-run disequilibrium must be prepared to confront not merely the manifestations of depression but also, more significantly, the sources of contagion per se.

Expansionist spending performs the very useful service of mitigating the social consequences of unemployed resources. Its capacity for prompt relief makes it a most valuable device, indeed. As indicated, such measures will undoubtedly constitute an essential part of any longer-run program as well. It is therefore indispensable that an integrated economic program be evolved to serve as the basis of any attack upon depressions. The formulation of a many-sided recovery plan should mitigate the dominance of the general expedient of public spending.

[10] These problems will be examined in some further detail in the following chapter.

LESSONS OF NEW DEAL SPENDING

EMERGENCY PUBLIC WORKS

We have neglected thus far a discussion of the objects of expenditure. The works projects of the thirties must be judged disappointing on the whole, with the exception of the PWA and various special projects, such as the TVA. The enterprises of the period partook to a distressing degree of emergency relief type of operations—relatively far removed from the category of regular public works projects. The federal government's pursuance of a work relief program has necessarily exerted a dominant influence on the pattern of projects selected.

Of the total number of workmen engaged in public construction, a major proportion is now accounted for by those who have been employed because they badly needed jobs to do, rather than because the job to be done needed them. . . . Out of that change have come related changes in the manner of doing work, such as the change from a maximization of labor-saving machinery to achieve greatest economy in construction operations to a maximization of the use of unskilled labor, and in the criteria of project selection, from placing major emphasis upon urgency of community demand to major emphasis upon a project's suitability for operation under work-relief auspices. The distribution of expenditures among the various purposes for which public improvements are constructed, however, is still not determined with the object of achieving a properly planned balance, except insofar as the distribution achieved expresses a balance of the immediate demands for various types of work.[11]

It has also been demonstrated that a series of "emergency" programs of public works construction may be self-defeating in achieving the aim of employment stabilization. Throughout the entire period discussed, there was no definitely continuing policy to guide the planners and administrators of federal, state, or local governments. Each program was set up as if it were the last. The consequence was a sort of "dead-line" type of administration, with projects chosen for prosecution in accordance with their degree of readiness and the quickness with which they would put great numbers of men to work, rather than in accordance with the urgency of demand for the improvement being undertaken. When these two criteria worked together, important and socially valuable community improvements resulted; when they conflicted, community value had to take second place.[12]

As earlier indicated,[13] various engineering considerations impose limitations upon the proper timing of a public works program. Most larger types of construction activity involve a relatively inflexible

---

[11] United States, National Resources Planning Board, *Development of Resources and Stabilization of Employment in the United States*, pp. 31–32.
[12] *Ibid.*, pp. 18–19.   [13] *Ibid.*, pp. 15–17.

period for completion and cannot, without considerable additional cost, be abandoned while in process and revived at some subsequent date. While it is true that for the decade of the thirties as a whole cyclical considerations were of secondary importance, the speed with which projects could be inaugurated proved to be a most vital consideration. In the absence of adequate public works planning, the administrative delays incidental to starting major projects tended to encourage greater participation in numerous smaller-scale projects, frequently of inferior quality.

The PWA program, especially in its early stages, was harassed by time-consuming administrative delays which threatened the entire plan. These delays were pronounced in connection with that portion of the program involving grants supporting locally sponsored projects. Usually many months elapsed between the authorization of a project and the time dirt began to fly, and many months more before any approximation of maximum-scale employment was realized. In the absence of advance planning, much time was necessarily consumed in the development of detailed plans and specifications, arranging to finance a project, acquiring land, advertising and passing upon bids, organizing construction operations, and establishing the relief qualifications of workers. Local financing sometimes involved the holding of special elections to approve the proposed bond issue.[14] The WPA program was confronted with much the same range of problems.

Turning to the construction activity of the federal government, we find that total operations, including direct expenditures, grants, loans, and guarantees, have expanded almost twenty times between the predepression period and 1940. Outlays have risen from a relatively fixed figure of about $200 million a year for the decade prior to the depression to a height of $3.4 billion in 1939. Expenditure for roads and streets leads the list of projects (in good part because of the relatively limited nonlabor costs entailed), with government plant which includes public buildings, educational buildings, recreation facilities, and publicly owned electric utilities second in importance in actual expenditure.

Despite the great increase in federal participation in the construction field, total public works expenditures have not risen materially over the predepression level. To a large degree federal grants replaced the reduced outlays made by local governments. It appears

[14] *Ibid.*, p. 20.

Chart VI

Expenditures for Construction of Federal Public Works Classified according to Function, Fiscal Years 1921–1941 [a]

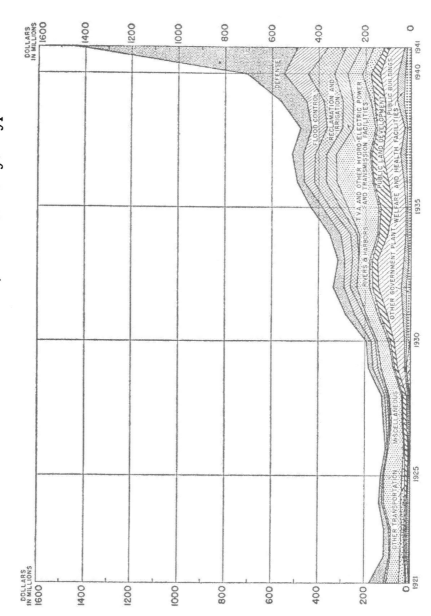

[a] Source: *Development of Resources and Stabilization of Employment in the United States*, Chart VII, p. 26. Prepared in the office of the National Resources Planning Board.

that state and local governments, in failing to increase their expenditures relative to the improvement in their fiscal abilities, took advantage of the expanded scope of federal operations. In 1940—when their capacity to undertake such activity was no longer impaired by financial difficulties—their scale of expenditures was far below that undertaken prior to the depression. The experience of the depression reveals the prime importance of co-ordinating the construction operations of the different governmental layers.

Long-range programming of local construction, in conformance with the long-range financial resources of the community, will go far toward smoothing out the curve of local public works activity, and will provide a sound basis of administration for any federal financial assistance to be made available during periods of depression. But the relations that are to prevail between the federal government and the state and local governments during an "emergency" period must be formulated in advance if the necessary coordination of action is to be achieved.[15]

PUBLIC AND PRIVATE CONSTRUCTION

Private construction activity has normally assumed far greater proportions than public operations. Thus, a sharp reduction in total private construction obliges a great proportionate expansion of public activity if aggregate construction outlays are to be maintained. During the decade of the twenties the ratio of public to private construction was roughly $2 billion (public) to $7 billion (private). In the years 1933–1940 this ratio (including public loans and loan guarantees) became slightly more than $2 billion (public) to $3 billion (private). Total public construction would have had to rise about $4 billion a year over the expenditures actually made during the years 1933–1940 to maintain the total volume of construction of the twenties. While some question may arise as to the existence of opportunities for an annual public investment in regular public projects of $6 billion or thereabouts, the adoption of a large-scale residential construction problem would have helped provide investment outlets of this magnitude. No program of such size, however, was ever seriously considered by the Roosevelt administration. The following chart shows the relative importance of private to public construction activity.

Public construction cannot provide employment for all the unemployed in periods of deep depression. Only a fraction of the unem-

[15] *Ibid.*, p. 18.

Chart VII

Estimated Volume of New Construction Activity in the United States, and Federal Expenditures and Guaranties for New Construction, 1920–1940 [a]

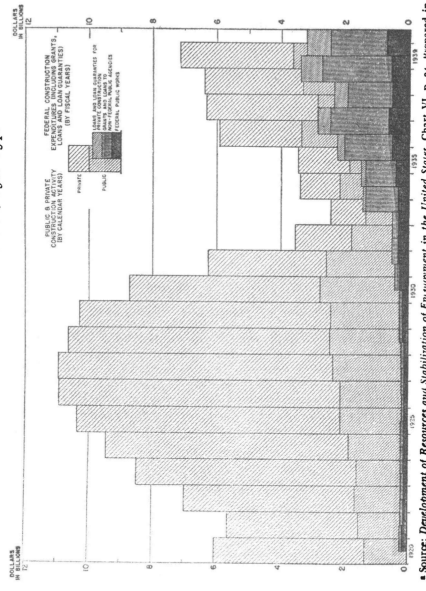

[a] Source: *Development of Resources and Stabilization of Employment in the United States*, Chart VI, p. 24. Prepared in the office of the National Resources Planning Board.

ployed possess the abilities and training required by regular public works activity. In the years 1932–1934 perhaps only 25 percent of the twelve to fourteen million unemployed could have been absorbed in a works program conducted at normal efficiency levels. While it is practicable to train additional construction workers, definite limits exist as to the number which could thus profitably be absorbed.[16] The scale assumed by emergency public works should not be made independent of a longer-run evaluation of a desirable pattern of total resource and labor allocation. It is imperative that public construction projects be appraised in the light of the contribution made to the development of the nation rather than as an excuse for providing employment. While it is incontestable that employment upon second-rate projects is superior to no employment at all, it should be the function of the federal government to assure a happier alternative. This, we contend, can be implemented by a positive orientation toward the private sector of the economy.

SELF-LIQUIDATING PUBLIC PROJECTS

Within the area of public construction operations considerable discussion has been devoted to the relative scope of self-liquidating to nonself-liquidating projects. Concern over the size of national indebtedness has prompted many to favor the former category at the expense of the latter. As earlier observed, the application of a pricing system to the distribution of public services must necessarily be limited, since a portion of the community would otherwise inevitably be deprived of some indispensable utilities. No one, for example, would seriously dispute the social and political desirability of our free educational institutions. Considerable difficulty, nevertheless, surrounds any precise determination of the proper scope of self-liquidating public enterprise. The answer here, however, is outside the province of this volume being essentially a political and social issue. We shall, therefore, restrict our discussion to more technical considerations arising out of the experience of the past decade.

The unsuccessful RFC "self-liquidating" loan program for local public works projects sponsored by President Hoover in 1932 has been submitted as evidence of the limited scope available for such

[16] See United States, *Works Projects Administration*, Division of Social Research, "Urban Workers on Relief," Research Monograph IV.

LESSONS OF NEW DEAL SPENDING

operations.[17] The conventional area of government commercial enterprise has been almost exclusively in the field of public utilities, including street railway systems and toll bridges. Street and highway development may also be included if the definition of "self-liquidating" is extended to include special taxes which may be enhanced—such as those on gasoline. This list is surely not impressive. The restricted scope for government activities that can be made wholly self-financing stems from our traditional exclusion of public enterprise from those fields entailing competition with private business. In Sweden, and in numerous other foreign countries where the state has played a vital entrepreneurial role, the opportunities for self-liquidating investment are consequently much greater.

While the prospects for wholly self-liquidating public investment are seriously limited, there are great opportunities for partially self-financing activity. For there exists a large area—chiefly in residential construction, hospitals, docks, and so forth—in which moderate public subsidies are capable of encouraging a considerable volume of new investment. In fact, it appears that perhaps the most fruitful field for a recovery program, proceeding primarily upon a public works plan, lies in residential construction. The excellent results derived from the limited activity in this field during the thirties may be viewed as evidence of the potential gains that can be realized. In retrospect it would seem that the administration erred seriously in assigning such a small role to expenditures in home construction.

The favor found by self-liquidating projects has, no doubt, been powerfully influenced by the fact that such enterprises are taken as *prima facie* assurance of usefulness—as contrasted with the frequently deficient character of nonself-liquidating operations. This prejudice can be combated most effectively by a judicious selection of regular public works projects. It is dangerous and lamentable indeed that a public works program be open to the criticism of boondoggling and general wastefulness.

[17] "The scheme was doomed to failure by the sheer lack of enough local projects capable of being financed on the toll bridge principle. By the end of 1933 the RFC had disbursed little more than $60 million for such projects (of the $1.5 billion so appropriated)" United States, National Resources Planning Board, *Development of Resources and Stabilization of Employment*, p. 15.

SUMMARY

The lessons to be found in the spending programs of the great depression are threefold: (1) A lasting recovery must be based upon a valid diagnosis and correction of the many elements contributing to prolonged economic stagnation. (2) Expansionist spending constitutes an essential factor in a recovery program, since (*a*) it permits immediate alleviation of the social consequences of depression, and (*b*) it operates as a hypodermic and may, if properly executed, speed up the recovery. (3) Emergency public spending, to be successful, must be co-ordinated with a consistent tax program, be based upon prepared project plans, and consist of worth-while additions to the national wealth. Compensatory spending policy is not *the* answer to unemployed resources, but it can and must play an important role in assisting more fundamental changes looking toward fuller—if not full—employment of resources.

VIII. PUBLIC SPENDING AND POSTWAR ECONOMIC POLICY

INTRODUCTION

As THE OUTLOOK for a United Nations victory grows brighter, the concern of the democratic peoples of the earth over the shape of the postwar world is sharpened. The pessimism rooted in the dismal decade of the thirties asserts itself in poignant apprehension over the future. Our failure to solve the problems of the last decade provides small assurance to the common man that the brave new world that science declares is within our grasp will be realized. Implicit in the advent of peace is the threat of the outbreak of depression. The democratic way of life cannot yet boast among its virtues the promise of freedom from want and the assurance of employment for all. Without these fundamental elements the fabric of democracy is tenuous indeed. The life span of our prized institutions may well depend upon the measure with which the legitimate economic aspirations of the populace are fulfilled.

In approaching the problem of the role of fiscal policy in postwar economic policy we shall distinguish two periods: (1) the immediate short-run transition period in which the major problem is that of expediting the shift of resources from war to civilian production, and (2) the long-run problem of providing full employment of resources. These two problems are obviously not entirely separate, and the manner in which the initial adjustment is effected will directly influence the prospects of a successful solution to the long-range problem of achieving an efficiently functioning economy.

THE SHORT-RUN PROBLEM

Some perspective of what the immediate termination of the war will mean may be gathered from statistics of the distribution of the gross national product. As shown in Table 5, the total portion of the gross national income attributable to governmental goods and services (war as well as normal activities), will amount to almost 60 percent in 1943. This proportion is more than three times as great as that experienced in 1939. Total federal expenditures for the fiscal year 1944 are expected to equal $113.5 billion, with war outlays accounting for $97 billion. While military appropriations in the postwar years are scheduled to drop greatly, they are likely to be appreciably larger than the level realized prior to 1939; aggregate federal expenditures in the years immediately after the war may be as high as $28-$38 billion. It is probable that there will occur only a gradual decline in outlays during the first six or nine months after the cessation of hostilities, with the greatest drop in such expenditures postponed until a year after this initial period, as was true of the last war.

TABLE 5

DISTRIBUTION OF GROSS NATIONAL PRODUCT [a]

(Percent of annual total)

	1939	1941	1942	1943
Gross national product	100.0	100.0	100.0	100.0 [b]
Goods and services for Government use (including State and local)	17.1	20.6	41.0	57
Private gross capital formation	12.6	16.0	5.5	0
Goods and services available for consumers	70.3	63.4	53.5	43

[a] Source: *Survey of Current Business*, February, 1943, p. 5.
[b] Estimated.

Within a year and a half or two, military appropriations are likely to fall between $70 and $80 billion below the forecast figure of $97 billion for the fiscal year 1944.[1] This will mean an annual federal budget of from $28 to $38 billion in the two years after the war. The above appropriation estimates assume large military outlays ranging from $17 to $27 billion and nonmilitary expenditures of $11 billion. These high military expenditures are not meant as predictions, but merely working hypotheses based upon the assumption that (1) we may wish to demobilize our armed forces slowly for political reasons relating to postwar territorial settlements; (2) we shall have sizable occupation forces in various parts of the world; (3) we shall wish to continue various parts of our projected military programs, especially our naval program; and (4) we shall attempt to avoid the dislocating impact of swift demobilization upon our domestic economy. The $11

[1] For our present purpose we have adopted the simplifying assumption that the expenditure figure for the fiscal year 1944 will not be exceeded in succeeding war budgets.

billion nonmilitary appropriation is based upon the average nonmilitary expenditure for the prewar fiscal years 1934–1940 of $7 billion plus an additional $4 billion annual interest burden.[2] It is probably safe to assume that in the event of a satisfactory peace settlement following the above emergency period, federal military appropriations are likely to fall considerably—to perhaps some $5 to $7 billion annually and [3] eventually much lower.

The immediate postwar problem may be viewed as involving the replacement of roughly $70 to $80 billion of federal war expenditures, with a corresponding volume of private expenditure. To maintain a national income of approximately $148 [4] billion will require more than $35 billion of gross capital formation.[5] A notion of the magnitude of the problem may be derived from comparison with the 1929 level of $20.3 billion gross capital formation which produced a gross national product of $93.6 billion.

It has been estimated that the termination of military operations will throw from 13 to 15 million persons, war workers and demobilized soldiers and sailors, upon the labor market.[6] This estimate is probably somewhat low, since the number of workers likely to be engaged in war industry before the end of 1943, as well as the scheduled size of our armed forces, exceeds Professor Hansen's figures.[7] The above consideration is, however, somewhat offset by our assumption that demobilization will be gradual and that our armed forces may number as large as two to four million during the first year or two after the war's end. We shall assume, as a point of departure, that "full employment" in the two or three postwar years

[2] It has been assumed that the federal debt reaches a total of $250 billion by the end of the war. Assuming, further, interest payments at the rate of 2 percent, we derive an annual interest bill of $5 billion—or some $4 billion above the 1934–1940 average.

[3] It is interesting to note that current statements of postwar goals, unlike those made during the last war, specifically omit references to the desirability of disarmament on the part of the victors. Considerable support appears to exist for an international police force to deal with aggressor nations.

[4] Estimate for 1943 by the National Income Section of the Department of Commerce.

[5] Based upon the ratios established by Simon Kuznets in his two reports, *National Income and Capital Formation, 1919–1935*, New York National Bureau of Economic Research, 1937, pp. 8, 40, and *Commodity Flow and Capital Formation in the Recent Recovery and Decline, 1932–38*, New York, National Bureau of Economic Research, 1939. It is difficult to infer from these studies as to the consequences of differences in the price level upon the above ratios.

[6] Alvin H. Hansen and Guy Greer "Toward Full Use of Our Resources," *Fortune*, XXVI, No. 5 (November, 1942), 130–133, 158–178. The authors estimate the total number of persons to be immediately released at the close of the war as between 18 and 21 million with some 5 to 6 million voluntarily retiring from the labor market after such time.

[7] *Ibid.*, p. 131.

(which may be estimated as the length of the transition stage between war and peace),[8] will require approximately $30 billion of gross capital formation (private and public) and the re-employment of perhaps 15 million persons.[9]

The postwar problem involves much more than returning to the pre-1939 economic level for, as already indicated, we were burdened at that time with substantial unutilized resources both human and physical. Furthermore, as a result of the war effort we have made great additions to our productive capacity as well as witnessed great strides in production techniques and man-hour output. To maintain full utilization of our built-up capital plant and provide employment for our increased labor force, we must aim, not at a goal of $80 to $90 billion national income, which would have appeared relatively ambitious prior to the war, but at an objective of from $110 to $120 billion as measured in prewar prices.

THE PROSPECTS

What are the immediate prospects after the war's close for the realization of a national income of this size? Before undertaking any analysis of this problem, it is pertinent to note some of the chief difficulties surrounding the reconversion of industry to civilian production. Priorities and concentration of industrial facilities have eliminated thousands of small and medium-size business concerns and numerous larger corporations which have not been able or were not given an opportunity to accept war orders. Many such concerns will not have the requisite capital with which to return to business, while others will be obliged to return to their former fields on a more limited scale.[10] Extensive industrial training will be required to prepare war workers for new civilian tasks. The redistribution of our working population during the war to areas previously unimportant industrially raises the problem of an adequate labor supply in the older industrial sections.

---

[8] Redvers Opie in a talk delivered before the American Marketing Association, reported that some English industries estimate they may require three years to reconvert to peacetime production. *New York Times*, February 26, 1943.

[9] It will be noted that we have followed Hansen's assumption that the majority of war workers will be relatively quickly absorbed through reconversion of industry to civilian production.

[10] In Great Britain it has been proposed that special provision be made to accommodate re-entry so as to avoid handicapping such firms relative to concerns in the same field that have managed to persevere.

Much special-purpose ordnance machinery will become worthless, and many time-consuming alterations will have to be made in newly constructed war plants before they are suitable for civilian production.

A major source of difficulty in the postwar period is in prospect as a result of the markedly uneven rates of technological efficiency realized within particular industries. Concerns not enjoying large war orders will be at a disadvantage compared to those firms which have been encouraged by great contracts to exploit technological innovations to the utmost. While war contracts have permitted and encouraged the output of producers subject to wide variations in cost, postwar conditions will not be so kind to high-cost firms. A return to any approximation of competitive markets will deal harshly with marginal concerns.

The immediate postwar economic environment will be shaped significantly by the deferred demand built up during the war years, as was true of World War I. Insofar as our economy is devoting a larger portion of its output to military production than it did during the last war,[11] the accumulated backlog of demand will be all the greater. Professor Sumner H. Slichter [12] has listed the various factors contributing to deferred demands as follows: [13] (1) deferred housing demand of $3.7 billion; (2) deferred consumer durable goods of $8.7 billion; (3) deferred business construction and equipment of $5.2 billion; (4) deferred private maintenance for private plants and residences of $2 billion; (5) deferred consumers' nondurable goods of $3 billion; (6) deferred regular public works of $1.8 billion, and (7) deferred public maintenance estimated at $600 million. The aggregate total of deferred demand resulting from the above sources equals $25 billion.

The world, as Slichter points out, will be confronted by the greatest shortages in history at the end of the war. The enormous domestic deferred demand estimated above will probably be exceeded considerably by foreign shortages attributable to both postponed consumer and producer demand plus the necessary replacement of wartime destruction. This figure is placed at roughly $40 billion. Domestic

---

[11] During the period of our participation in World War I; approximately 25 percent of the total national output was absorbed in military production.

[12] See "Postwar Boom or Collapse," *Harvard Business Review*, XXI (autumn, 1942), 5-42.

[13] The calculations submitted have been based upon the hypothesis that the war will end in June, 1944.

surplus liquid assets in the form of war bonds or cash, in excess of the amount individuals will probably wish to hold, are estimated by Slichter as totaling perhaps more than $40 billion by June, 1944. The rest of the world, however, will be far less favorably situated with respect to its ability to meet the great postwar shortages. Most foreign nations will face the problems of peacetime reconstruction with seriously weakened financial structures and impaired capital equipment. Upon the United States, consequently, will devolve the greatest single responsibility for foreign postwar rehabilitation.

Further sources of prospective demand are noted by Professor Slichter in the probable great rise in the marriage rate with the consequent growth in demand for housing and household furnishings; the cumulative backlog of new businesses frustrated during the war years; the demand for housing and public utilities resulting from wartime population shifts, especially to the west and the south, and finally the great impetus to be expected from the varied technological advances of recent years. Technological progress has been enormously stimulated by the war and many industrial advances, moreover, will have to wait for the war's close before finding expression.

The promise of technological changes in materials, techniques, and products is rich indeed. We appear to be on the threshold of vast revolutionary developments that are likely to alter profoundly the world in which we live. Many of these innovations, such as the family plane and popular consumption of television sets, will probably not assume significant proportions until well after the transition period. Other developments, however, such as prefabricated or partly prefabricated housing, greatly expanded transoceanic freight and passenger service, vastly improved passenger automobiles, and widespread use of plastics, are likely to play an important role in the immediate postwar period.[14]

Professor Slichter's general conclusion, based on the foregoing considerations, is most optimistic for the prospect of prosperous conditions in the postwar years. Concern is manifest, however, over the danger of inflation in the absence of adequate price-control measures.[15] Another source of difficulty is seen in the high prewar corporate tax structure.[16]

[14] See the Appendix "Technology and Postwar Life" to the *Fortune* magazine supplement for Vol. XXVI, No. 6 (December, 1942), "The United States in a New World."

[15] Demand deposits, assuming reasonably effective price control, are likely to rise, he predicts, perhaps $15 or $20 billion by 1944.

[16] "Even before the war Federal taxes had become so high that they were determining the outlook for profits." "Postwar Boom or Collapse," p. 35.

POSTWAR ECONOMIC POLICY

Despite the above persuasive recital, the transition period is not likely to be as smooth or as happy as is suggested. We have previously noted several sources of difficulty relating to reconversion to peacetime production. The shift to civilian markets will not be accomplished over night, nor will there be merely isolated business casualties. The rise of new war-stimulated industrial areas is likely to produce serious distress in the older industrial centers. The industrial decline of New England states after the last war will probably be duplicated, in part, for this and other manufacturing and commercial regions.

Reconversion unemployment promises to be very substantial during the first two postwar years. Any precise calculation here is obviously impossible. It is not improbable, however, that unemployment from this source may range from five to ten million in the first postwar year. In the event, for instance, that the automobile industry were to decide to junk its 1942 tools and dies and start from scratch upon a radically new model, peak production may be delayed as much as two years or more. The British estimate of three years for the reconversion progress for several industries is disheartening. Furthermore, the race for reconversion, in addition to raising the threat of inflation in the acute form experienced after the last war, will probably engender materials hoarding and associated practices unless controlled by the government. The reluctance to convert to war production manifested by numerous corporations will not be duplicated in the reverse direction. Rather, it is certain that every device will be utilized to speed reconversion. This is obviously most desirable, but it gives rise to an inflationary movement which may be most difficult to prevent.

PUBLIC POLICY IN THE TRANSITION PERIOD

Government policy in the transition period will necessarily concern itself with the following immediate problems: (1) achieving an orderly demobilization, with ample regard for industry's capacity to absorb man power; (2) control over the flow of materials to assure the most satisfactory distribution of materials as an aid to rapid reconversion; (3) anticipation of the great inflationary pressure by adequate fiscal and other controls; (4) adoption of a large-scale labor training program to facilitate early reconversion; (5) execution of a prepared program of essential public works in close co-operation with state and local governments; (6) development of a program designed to extend financial aid to distressed corporations and expedite the re-entry of firms forced out of business during the war; [17] (7) provision of unemployment insurance and other social security benefits beyond the statutory period until such time as new employment opportunities are available.

The probable volume and duration of the unemployment problem in the transition period is most difficult to predict. The size of the problem will depend in large part upon the rate of demobilization adopted in relation to the rate of reconversion achieved by industry. If the former proceeds at a greater pace than industry's capacity to absorb man power, unemployment will naturally materialize. It would be most advantageous (although probably not politically feasible) if demobilization plans were synchronized with the probable reconversion periods for different industries. The latter could probably be calculated with some degree of precision. Some form of selective demobilization providing for the release of members of the armed forces with due consideration of the prevailing labor market for different types of skill could aid in reducing the volume of unemployment.

As earlier described, the accumulated deferred demand of consumers and producers is certain to assume enormous proportions. There will be a vast market for an endless variety of products. Production, in the period following the war's close, will for many lines probably be pushed to capacity levels. Inflationary pressures, as was true after World War I, will be most threatening during this period. It is imperative, therefore, that OPA price ceilings shall not be abandoned and that such controls be supplemented by an efficiently functioning system of fiscal devices in which tax rates on income earned at the source can be promptly adjusted. Finally, a restrictive banking policy constitutes the third indispensable adjunct to an effective repulse of the postwar inflationary threat.

Substantial reconversion unemployment will in all likelihood be experienced in the first two years after the war's end. This unemployment promises to be paralleled by great inflationary pressures. Assuming the above conditions, what provisions should be made for the unemployed? How feasible will a large-scale public works program be in the environment assumed above?

As earlier noted, one of the major prospective sources of new investment and employment opportunities lies in the field of residential

[17] Considerable caution will have to be exercised in determining the extent to which various concerns should be encouraged to re-enter their earlier fields.

construction. The pace of new construction activity, for several years perhaps, promises to be limited only by the availability of skilled labor and materials. The existence of a major public works program which competed for labor and materials with private demand would contribute to an inflationary price movement on the one hand and to a reduction in the scale of private construction activities on the other. If the foregoing hypothesis of postwar conditions in the building field is correct, government activity in this area should be restricted to essential operations. In the event that the foregoing estimate proves too optimistic, the scope of public construction will accordingly need to be expanded.

The expected housing boom will, however, probably not reach down to the lower-income groups, where self-liquidating construction is financially impossible. The housing accommodations available will improve somewhat as the result of the vacancies created by the movement of middle-income groups into new residences. It is difficult, however, to calculate the degree of relief afforded lower-income groups by new construction. To some extent the housing market is a discontinuous one. High vacancy rates for middle-income housing have not infrequently existed alongside serious shortages in housing facilities for low-income groups. Then, too, new residential reconstruction may be undertaken in areas removed from prevailing shortages for low-income housing. These considerations forcibly raise the issue of the desirable extent of federal participation in residential construction.

It has been estimated, according to various standards, that "from four to seven million non-farm dwelling units are unfit for habitation, or unhealthy to live in or sub-standard. A five year program for the replacement of these structures . . . would involve an annual construction volume of 800,000 to 1,400,000 dwelling units . . ."[18] Such a program, which could proceed only on the basis of public subsidies, would serve to reduce substantially the scale of private self-liquidating residential construction—since the facilities of the construction industry would temporarily be saturated. The seriousness of the above low-income housing situation will, of course, be relieved in part by new nonsubsidized housing construction. A certain volume of publicly subsidized residential building, under private or public auspices, will have to be undertaken. The precise scope of such operations will

[18] Leo Grebler, "Housing Policy and the Building Cycle," *Review of Economic Statistics*, XXIV (May, 1942), 68.

necessarily be determined by: (1) the volume and character of private construction; (2) the criteria adopted in determining substandard housing; (3) an evaluation of the desirability of temporarily expanding the relative size of the construction industry and the number of workers so occupied; (4) the rate of reconversion effected in the industries engaged in building-material supplies as against other industries; and (5) by the existence or nonexistence of long-range public works plans.

The largest portion of the unemployed in the transition period will have to be protected by unemployment insurance benefits. Such aid will have to be extended to cover the time required by industry to reconvert its resources to peacetime production.

The statutory unemployment benefit period will have to be extended, and weekly payments adjusted upward wherever necessary. Such extra-insurance payments should come from the Treasury so as to protect the status of social security funds. Due to the existence of the social security program and considerable savings in the form of war savings bonds, the plight of unemployed workers should be eased considerably—in the event that employment is found within a reasonably short time. No such cushion, however, will be available in many cases for returning members of our armed forces. It will obviously be imperative to afford them benefits at least equal to those available to civilian war workers. This can be achieved most expeditiously, perhaps, by extending to them the benefits of the Social Security Act, again to be financed from general funds. The cost of the above plan may vary from $1 billion to $3 billion or more in the first postwar year. The rate of demobilization adopted will largely determine the costs involved.[19]

In summary, the transitional period is likely to be characterized by a considerable volume of reconversion unemployment on the one hand and great inflationary pressures on the other. While investment opportunities promise to be extensive, numerous impediments confront the free flow of capital. The character of some of the more important problems has been noted, and suggestions have been offered for their alleviation. The nature of the discussion has inevitably suffered because of the exclusion of longer-run considerations.

[19] The costs entailed by an extension of unemployment insurance benefits have not been added to the $11 billion annual nonmilitary expenditure figure assumed for the transition period. Since there has been assumed a possible range of $10 billion in military outlays, the unemployment insurance subsidy may be viewed as subordinate and deductible from this larger outlay.

THE POST-TRANSITIONAL PERIOD

We now turn to the post-transitional period for an examination of some of the more fundamental elements affecting the level of national income and the role which may be allocated to public spending policy. Our analysis of the obstacles to long-run prosperity has stressed the inhibiting contribution of market imperfections and restrictive trade and labor practices. The importance of psychological considerations, particularly the general character of the relations existing between business and the federal government and the vital role exercised by the tax system, has been noted. The maintenance of a high level of consumer purchasing power has been deemed essential to the achievement of prosperous conditions. Fiscal policy has been assigned the residual task of providing employment for resources not otherwise occupied. The details of such a program will be discussed subsequently. The other major task relates to the reconstruction of international economic relations. Not only will prewar political and economic conflicts have to be resolved, but it is imperative that the leading nations of the world participate collectively in planning for optimum resource use.

The importance of establishing a more efficiently functioning price system has not escaped the attention of the Roosevelt administration.[20] Prior to our entrance into the war, the Department of Justice, under the leadership of Thurman Arnold, was engaged in a vigorous program of antitrust prosecutions. Mr. Arnold was pledged to a piecemeal attack of the problem of price rigidities in its varied forms. The Sherman Act was held to be broad enough to provide a basis for a comprehensive attack upon all the virulent forms of monopolistic market imperfections. Mr. Arnold's prosecutions, however, revealed a relatively unsophisticated interpretation of monopoly elements as indicated in the following statement:

The great mass of our population sell their goods, services and labor in a competitive market. They buy their necessities in a controlled market. Thus our economic structure consists of two separate worlds. The first is a world of organized industry; the second is a world of small unorganized businessmen, farmers, laborers and consumers.[21]

[20] President Roosevelt in his "Message on Monopolies," of April 29, 1938, declared: "One of the primary causes of our present (economic) difficulties lies in the disappearance of price competition in many industrial fields, particularly in basic manufacture where concentrated economic power is most evident—and where rigid prices and fluctuating payrolls are general."

[21] *The Bottlenecks of Business*, p. 12.

Mr. Arnold, interestingly enough, presents as his exhibit A of competition, the automobile industry—a field which has long been dominated by nonprice competition.

The record of antitrust prosecutions [22] reveals feeble accomplishments to date. Not only is the Sherman Act obsolete, but so is much of the legal orientation to modern market phenomena.[23] The most widespread type of restrictive price behavior, and by far the most pernicious in its impact upon economic behavior, is "imperfect competition." The legal disregard of this common form of trade restraint speaks strongly of the vitality of the trust-busting heritage. Any movement seeking to modify such practices as price agreements, price leadership, market sharing, limitation of competition, and control of prices through trade associations, price rigidities, fictitious product differentiation, and so forth, must operate within a much larger frame of reference than the Sherman Act.

The clumsy instrument of Antitrust needs to be fashioned to its gigantic task.... If litigation must continue to be the instrument of public policy, it ... [must] enjoy, an easier, speedier, more certain process, less freighted with procedures, less confused by the irrelevancies of legalism. It needs to borrow a bit of directness and dispatch from the world of business within which it must operate.[24]

The ordinary process of litigation, however, is inadequate for the huge job of operating over the largest portion of the American economy. Far superior to litigation in the necessary case-by-case approach is the device of the administrative rule. The informal procedure applicable in the sphere of negotiation provides a speedy instrument of control. The adoption of the technique of administrative review and ruling is ideally designed to handle the infinitely complex pattern of business practices which occupies the limbo between competition and monopoly. The agency entrusted with such a great responsibility must develop a system of rules appropriate to a highly dynamic economy. This is a task more for the professional economist, perhaps, than for the legal mind. For the ultimate test in every case is the consonance of business practice with the most effective utilization of resources.

The great variety of market situations revealed by the TNEC in-

---

[22] See Appendix to United States, Temporary National Economic Committee, *Monograph No. 16:* "Antitrust in Action," by Walton Hamilton and Irene Till.

[23] "A group, whose craft is litigation rather than industrial control, has made it (Sherman Act) the instrument that it is." Monograph No. 16. *Ibid.*, p. 35.

[24] *Ibid.*, p. 105.

vestigations [25] emphasizes the complexity of business relationships. It has been impossible for the TNEC to advocate uniform price policies for industry as a whole.[26] What is desired is not unrestrained competition, with its attendant high bankruptcy rate, but something between pure competition and various forms of quasi-monopoly. The most acceptable criteria would seem to be the lowest level of prices consistent with an adequate profit margin. J. M. Clark's formula that prices should be high enough to cover the costs of a representative firm and yield a return sufficient to attract needed capital can be accepted as a tentative yardstick.[27]

The revitalization of capitalist enterprise is a vast undertaking; it is beyond the province of this volume to explore in detail the numerous changes called for in our ailing economy. The above recommendations for purging the market of some of its enervating elements are not presumed to represent more than a partial corrective. A successful approach will have to embody many lines of procedure combining positive, as well as negative, action. Part of the program entails educational and propaganda activity seeking the conversion of businessmen to constructive market and pricing policies. No publicly sponsored movement aimed at the reconstruction of market practices can succeed without the co-operative assistance of business itself. For the unregenerated businessman can always be relied upon to invent new loopholes to circumvent the objectives of any such program.

The responsibility of organized labor with respect to the attainment of an efficiently functioning market mechanism is not less than that of business itself, although the pattern of co-operation to be secured in this sphere is far from patent. As an initial objective, the elimination of the various "featherbed" and other practices antithetical to optimum output can be claimed as the legitimate contribution of labor. The writer is aware of no simple solution to the perplexing problem of wage-rate determination. The uneconomic wage levels prevalent in the building trades have been noted, and a tentative basis for renegotiation has been suggested (annual wage guarantees). The pious hope may be expressed that the development of a well-organized and responsible labor movement may facilitate wage determination

---

[25] See *Monograph No. 21*, "Competition and Monopoly in American Industry," by Clair Wilcox.

[26] See Final Report of the Executive Secretary to the United States, Temporary National Economic Committee.

[27] *Social Control of Business*, p. 130.

consistent with principles governing the full use of resources. The ignorance of the role of satisfactory cost-price relationships in total income determination has been no more pronounced on the part of labor leaders than of business executives in general. Upon the federal government, hence, is thrown a great educational and administrative responsibility. Management-labor clinics, assisted by government experts, can perform a great service in assisting in the resolution of business and labor policies in a fashion most consistent with optimum output.

In the sphere of taxation a complete overhauling of our revenue system is in order. Our revenue structure has, like Topsy, "just growed," without any mature consideration for its impact upon consumption on the one hand and the flow of savings on the other. A review of the entire federal revenue system is called for in the light of such factors as the desirable disposition of income between savings and expenditures and the flow of funds to new investment. Especially vital is the determination of the functions served by various types of business taxation and the extent to which they duplicate features of the personal income tax system.

THE ROLE OF PUBLIC SPENDING

It has already been suggested that public spending can most appropriately fulfill a residual function rather than be assigned a primary responsibility in assuring full use of resources. The required scale of spending operations will reflect the effectiveness of the other segments of economic policy. It is obviously impossible to forecast at this time the long-run trend of postwar national income. The margin of idle resources over a number of years may be insignificant or it may assume substantial proportions. In the latter event, a spending program confined to conventional categories of outlay may prove deficient, due to the limited avenues for public investment. The thesis that the future will necessarily be deficient of adequate profitable investment outlets has been disputed. However, it would be unrealistic indeed to assume uninterrupted prosperity, even in the event of the attainment of optimum institutional adjustment. No doubt the postwar economic environment will be far short of that.

Proposals for public works programs in recent years have been primarily oriented toward long-range, continuing projects designed for the dual objective of building up and of protecting our national re-

POSTWAR ECONOMIC POLICY 155

sources and capital, and secondly, to provide employment for idle productive capacity and man power.[28] Cyclical considerations have been subordinated to the more basic alleged problem of secular stagnation. Public works projects cannot be assigned major responsibility for meeting short-term unemployment. This problem is more properly the province of an unemployment insurance program. This latter instrument would provide a much more flexible medium than that afforded by any public works program. To provide the most effective aid to the unemployed, the statutory benefit periods may have to be liberalized. The formation of a short-run public works program will have to be based upon full appreciation of the complementary relationships involved.

The National Resources Planning Board has prepared excellent detailed programs for regional resource development. The great majority of the proposed projects are eminently desirable—independent of the incidental employment creation—and should be executed substantially as recommended. In a recent National Planning Association Pamphlet, *Regional Resource Development*,[29] it is estimated that "a thorough-going developmental program would entail a public investment of some $2 billion per year for the next generation." [30] The projects reviewed are additional to the category of regular public works. The above program is viewed as a continuing enterprise rather than a reserve stock of projects available for recession contingencies. Of the following classes of water and land development projects, (1) flood control, (2) irrigation and reclamation, (3) public land development, (4) rivers and harbors, and (5) power generation and distribution, only No. 5 involves competition with private enterprise.

Public competition in the field of utilities should act as a healthy catalytic agent, spurring on technological innovation and challenging review of the prevailing pricing practices.[31] The TVA, for example,

[28] See United States, National Resources Planning Board studies: *Development of Resources and Stabilization of Employment in the United States*, and *National Resources Development—Report for 1942*.
[29] *Regional Resource Development*, by Alvin H. Hansen and Harvey S. Perloff.
[30] *Ibid.*, p. 35.
[31] "The real problem of the utilities is not who owns them, but how, in the absence of competition, to keep them on their toes. Monopolies are not proof against technological competition, as the railroads learned; but they are peculiarly given to technological sloth. Neither regulation, private ownership, nor public ownership is an adequate substitute for competition. Probably the best practical substitute is to let the same old debates go on, with outside industries, the utility magnates, municipal plants, and an occasional TVA all harrying each other as needed." *Fortune* magazine, "The United States in a New World." Supplement for December, 1942, p. 10.

has had a regenerating influence throughout the public utilities field, especially in the southeast region. Abundant power, moreover, has had a signal effect upon the rate of growth of industrial activity of the entire neighboring area. The other classes of project listed above are all calculated to increase national productivity and purchasing power.

Such projects, however, can in a limited way be utilized as cyclical stabilizing devices. The hazards confronting a cyclical public works program arising from the unpredictability of the cycle and the unwieldiness of the larger type of project have been emphasized. The advance planning of total public works activity by the different levels of government can, as has been indicated, achieve substantial benefits. The mere existence of a continuous volume of public investment operations throughout the cycle may exercise a stabilizing influence on the course of economic activity.

Exclusive of federal activity in the field of residential construction, it is doubtful that a total public outlay of more than $4 to $5 billion a year can profitably be undertaken (regular plus regional developmental programs of the type listed above). The desirable level of governmental construction operations must be viewed in the light of some notion of optimum allocation of resources. While total public works outlays, exclusive of housing, could conceivably absorb several times the above expenditures, such a program would involve a great volume of uneconomic investment. There are limits beyond which the production of new roads and highways, bridges, irrigation projects, post offices, and so forth, becomes sheer waste. In the event that failure of private investment obliges a level of public investment beyond the legitimate needs for various regular public projects, new fields will have to be invaded. The entire public utilities and transportation fields offer great opportunities for useful public investment.

The conclusion is inescapable that definite limitations exist upon the scope of public investment in the accepted categories. If private enterprise fails to provide adequate investment outlets, it will have to suffer an invasion of its domain by the federal government—or else we will be reduced to building pyramids or equally useless projects. If the system of private enterprise is unable to achieve a high level of income there is small justification in limiting public projects to noncompetitive activity. The greatest contribution the government can make is in sponsoring the reconstruction of private enterprise along

POSTWAR ECONOMIC POLICY

competitive lines and providing a hospitable investment climate. This failing, private enterprise will inevitably be obliged to become subordinated to government control and investment.

Can we afford the costs entailed by a public construction program of the proportions described above? Can fiscal solvency be maintained with peacetime deficits adding to the $250–$300 billion odd debt level facing us at the war's close? The answer to the above queries, the writer believes, is in the affirmative. The wartime illustration that whatever is physically possible is financially possible is, within limits, also true in peacetime. The problem of an expanding debt and the determination of the relative scope of taxation on the one hand and deficits on the other is eminently a manageable one. A rising debt becomes a serious problem only when interest charges rise more rapidly than income and taxable capacity or when the need for additional revenue forces the adoption of taxes which discourage enterprise. Appropriate fiscal and banking controls can help eliminate exposure to inflation or financial insolvency. Private enterprise need not be plagued with self-induced apprehension over the consequences of planned budgetary deficits. Rather, such a program, when integrated with positive measures for the revitalization of business, fulfills a necessary and desirable complementary relationship. Our economic future and that of the rest of the world can be secure, indeed, if we are prepared to insist that full employment can be achieved by realistically facing the elements responsible for our prewar plight.

INTERNATIONAL ECONOMIC POLICY

The course of postwar economic life will be determined in appreciable measure by the international economic policies prosecuted by the United Nations, particularly the United States. In the postwar period this country will be in a position comparable to that occupied by England in the nineteenth century, when that nation was able to outproduce and outsell all competitors. Any effort on our part to assert our superior competitive situation will precipitate a wave of protectionism and discriminatory agreements and launch the world on the road to poverty and political conflict. If an international equilibrium consistent with the welfare of not only strong but also small and weaker nations is to be achieved, it can only be the product of clearsighted, international economic planning. It is in this realm that the United States faces its greatest challenge, for here exists the greatest disparity between nominal short-run gains and long-term welfare and international stability.

The pattern of postwar international trade is not likely to duplicate prewar experience.[32] Many countries have learned too well the hazards of specialization and can be counted upon to strive for the realization of improved internal economic balance. The disadvantageous trade position of agricultural nations relative to industrial countries so apparent since World War I and the more recent replacement by synthetics of natural products such as rubber, petroleum, textiles, and so forth will dictate a shift from regional specialization in the direction of regional balance.

The leading industrial nations can choose to impede this development or else they can co-operate wholeheartedly in assisting in its fulfillment. The denial of investment loans to backward nations will postpone their programs for internal reconstruction and result in low living standards and reduced volume of foreign trade. The achievement of a happy balance of exports and imports on the one hand and foreign loans on the other is a delicate task, indeed, and not one to be realized through the unplanned decisions of private traders and investors. The chronic shortage of dollars that continued to plague international trade and the football of competitive currency depreciation cannot be permitted to reappear. The flow of world trade and capital movements must be guided by considerations other than selfish profit. The direction of international economic reconstruction is most appropriately the province of a progressive United Nations committee. The welfare of the postwar world depends in no small part upon the intelligence with which some such group fulfills its tasks.

The United Nations, in full appreciation of the vital importance of expanding international trade, have already accepted the policy of multilateral trade and collective endeavor to secure higher living standards and social security. The development of backward areas assumes crucial significance in this perspective. The details of international economic reconstruction are outside the scope of this volume. However, it is appropriate to sketch briefly the outlines of the pattern of aid by industrially advanced nations to backward and young countries concerned with internal development. The following tentative suggestions may be offered.[33]

[32] See Kindleberger, "Planning for Foreign Investment," *American Economic Review*, XXXIII (Supplement, March, 1943), 347-354.
[33] After National Planning Association, *International Development Loans*.

1. The provision of international capital and technical assistance to countries interested in internal development programs—free from the odious implications of imperialism.

2. Loans should be extended under the direction of an international committee composed of representatives of debtor and creditor nations.

3. Loans extended by the international committee should be made at low rates of interest for periods up to 25 years. Amortization should be adopted wherever practicable out of the returns of the investment.

4. National subscription to the capital of the International Committee should be determined in accordance with the capacities of the member nations.

5. Foreign loans should also be extended to assist in the restoration of multilateral exchange markets.

We have contended that private enterprise complemented by public operations can offer investment outlets sufficient for prosperous conditions. The relative scope of public to private investment will be determined in large measure by the extent to which contemporary business and labor practices, among other things, are revitalized. Whether the host of pitfalls confronting the resurgence of private enterprise can be successfully surmounted remains to be seen. To this task must be devoted the collective effort of business, labor, and government. Above all, we cannot afford poverty, idleness, and their social and political concomitants.

BIBLIOGRAPHY

BOOKS

Adams, H. C. Science of Finance. New York, Holt and Company, 1924.

Angell, James W. Investment and Business Cycles. New York, McGraw-Hill, 1941.

Arnold, Thurman. The Bottlenecks of Business. New York, Reynal and Hitchcock, 1940.

Brookings Institution. National Recovery Administration. Washington, D.C., 1936.

Bullock, C. J. Politics Finance and Consequences. Cambridge, Mass., Harvard University Press, 1939.

—— Selected Readings in Public Finance. 2d ed., Boston, Ginn and Company, 1924.

Burns, A. E., and D. S. Watson. Government Spending and Economic Expansion. Washington, D.C., American Council on Public Affairs, 1940.

Burns, A. R. The Decline of Competition. New York, McGraw-Hill, 1936.

Cassel, Gustav. The Theory of Social Economy. London, T. Fisher, Unwin, 1923.

Chamberlin, Edward. The Theory of Monopolistic Competition. Cambridge, Mass., Harvard University Press, 1933.

Clark, J. M. The Economics of Planning Public Works. Washington, D.C., Government Printing Office, 1935.

—— Social Control of Business. New York, McGraw-Hill, 1939.

—— Strategic Factors in Business Cycles. New York, National Bureau of Economic Research, 1934.

Colm, Gerhard, and Fritz Lehmann. Economic Consequences of Recent American Tax Policy. New York, Social Research, 1938.

Crum, W. L., J. F. Fennelly, and L. H. Seltzer. Fiscal Planning for Total War. New York, National Bureau of Economic Research, 1942.

Dalton, Hugh, and others. Unbalanced Budgets. London, Routledge and Sons, 1934.

Eccles, Marriner S. Economic Balance and a Balanced Budget; collected public papers, ed. by R. L. Weissman, New York, Harper, 1940.

Economist (London). The New Deal. New York, Knopf, 1937.

Ezekiel, Mordecai. Jobs for All through Industrial Expansion. New York, Knopf, 1939.

Foster, W. T., and W. Catchings. Profits. Boston, Houghton Mifflin, 1925.

Gayer, Arthur D. Public Works in Prosperity and Depression. New York, National Bureau of Economic Research, 1935.

Gilbert, Richard V., and others. An Economic Program for American Democracy. New York, Vanguard Press, 1936.

Gourvitch, Alexander. Survey of Economic Theory on Technological Change and Employment. Philadelphia, Pa., United States, Work Projects Administration, National Research Project, 1940.
Great Britain, Poor Law Commission, Minority Report. London, His Majesty's Stationery Office, 1909.
Haberler, Gottfried von. Prosperity and Depression. Geneva, League of Nations, 1938; revised edition, 1941.
Hansen, Alvin H. Economic Stabilization in an Unbalanced World. New York, Harcourt, Brace, 1932.
―― Fiscal Policy and Business Cycles. New York, W. W. Norton, 1941.
―― Full Recovery or Stagnation? New York, W. W. Norton, 1938.
Hardy, C. O. Credit Policies of the Federal Reserve System. Washington, D.C., Brookings Institution, 1932.
Harris, Seymour E., ed. Postwar Economic Problems. New York, McGraw-Hill, 1943.
Harrod, R. F. The Trade Cycle. London, Oxford University Press, 1936.
Hart, A. G., and E. D. Allen. Paying for Defense. Philadelphia, The Blakiston Company, 1941.
Hayek, F. A. Prices and Production. Rev. ed. London, Macmillan, 1935.
―― Profits, Interest and Investment. London, Routledge and Sons, 1939.
Hicks, J. R. The Theory of Wages. London, Macmillan, 1935.
Hicks, Mrs. U. K. The Finance of British Government, 1920–1936. London, Oxford University Press, 1938.
Hill, A. C. C., and I. Lubin. The British Attack on Unemployment. Washington, D.C., The Brookings Institution, 1934.
International Labour Office. Public Works Policy; Studies and Reports, Series C (Employment and Unemployment). No. 19. Geneva, 1935.
Johnson, G. Griffith. The Treasury and Monetary Policy, 1933–1938. Cambridge, Mass., Harvard University Press, 1939.
Kalecki, Michael. Essays in the Theory of Economic Fluctuations. New York, Farrar and Rinehart, 1939.
Keynes, J. M. The General Theory of Employment, Interest and Money. New York, Harcourt, Brace, 1936.
―― How to Pay for the War. New York, Harcourt, Brace, 1940.
―― The Means to Prosperity. New York, Harcourt, Brace, 1933.
King, W. I. The National Income and Its Purchasing Power. New York, National Bureau of Economic Research, 1930.
―― The Wealth and Income of the People of the United States. New York, Macmillan, 1915.
Kuznets, Simon Smith. Commodity Flow and Capital Formation in the Recent Recovery and Decline, 1932–1938. New York, 1939. National Bureau of Economic Research, Publications, No. 34.
―― National Income and Capital Formation, 1919–1935. New York, 1937. National Bureau of Economic Research, Publications, No. 32.
League of Nations. Enquiry on National Public Works. Geneva, 1934.

BIBLIOGRAPHY

—— World Economic Surveys. Geneva, Annual volumes 1931–1932 through 1938–1939.
Lindahl, Erik R. Studies in the Theory of Money and Capital. London, Allen and Unwin, 1939.
Lundberg, Erik. Studies in the Theory of Economic Expansion. London, King and Son, 1937.
Madden, John J., Marcus Nadler, and H. C. Sauvain. America's Experience as a Creditor Nation. New York, Prentice-Hall, Inc., 1937.
Meade, J. E. An Introduction to Economic Analysis and Policy. London, Oxford University Press, 1937.
Mitchell, Wesley C. Business Cycles. New York, National Bureau of Economic Research, 1927.
Moulton, H. G. The Formation of Capital. Washington, D.C., Brookings Institution, 1935.
Myrdal, Gunnar. Monetary Equilibrium. London, William Hodges, 1939.
National Bureau of Economic Research. Business Cycles and Unemployment. New York, 1923.
—— Planning and Control of Public Works. New York, 1930.
Nugent, Rolf. Consumer Credit and Economic Stability. New York, Russell Sage Foundation, 1939.
Pigou, A. C. Economics of Welfare. 4th ed. London, Macmillan, 1933.
—— Employment and Equilibrium. London, Macmillan, 1941.
—— Socialism versus Capitalism. London, Macmillan, 1937.
—— The Theory of Unemployment. London, Macmillan, 1933.
Schumpeter, Joseph A. Business Cycles. 2 vols. New York, McGraw-Hill, 1939.
—— The Theory of Economic Development. Cambridge, Mass., Harvard University Press, 1934.
Shoup, Carl, and others. Facing the Tax Problem. New York, Twentieth Century Fund, 1937.
Simons, Henry C. Personal Income Taxation. Chicago, University of Chicago Press, 1938.
Slichter, Sumner H. Towards Stability. New York, Holt, 1935.
Smith, Adam. Wealth of Nations. Everyman's edition. New York, Dutton, 1910.
Smith, Dan T. Deficits and Depressions. New York, Wiley, 1936.
Social Science Research Council. Transcript of Proceedings of Conference at Rye, New York, on Alvin H. Hansen's preliminary report on Fiscal Policy and Business Cycles, June, 1939. Mimeographed.
Spiethoff, Arthur A. C. "Krisen," in Handwörterbuch de Staatswissenschaften, Vol. VI, 1925.
Stewart, Paul W., and Rufus E. Tucker. The National Debt and Government Credit. New York, Twentieth Century Fund, 1937.
Thomas, Brinley. Monetary Policy and Crises. London, Routledge and Sons, 1936.

BIBLIOGRAPHY

Tinbergen, J. Statistical Testing of Business Cycle Theories, I. Geneva, League of Nations, 1939.

Tungan-Baranowski, M. Les Crises industrielles en Angleterre. Paris, M. Giard and E. Briere, 1913.

United States, Department of Commerce. World Economic Review, Washington, D.C., Government Printing Office, 1933, 1934, 1935, and 1936.

United States, National Resources Committee. Consumer Income in the United States. Washington, D.C., Government Printing Office, 1939.

United States, National Resources Planning Board. Development of Resources and Stabilization of Employment in the United States. Washington, D.C., Government Printing Office, 1941.

—— The Economic Effects of the Federal Public Works Expenditures, 1933–1938. Washington, D.C., Government Printing Office, 1940.

—— National Resources Development-Report for 1942. Washington, D.C., Government Printing Office, 1942.

—— Consumer Expenditures in the United States. Washington, D.C., Government Printing Office, 1939.

United States, Temporary National Economic Committee. Monographs. Washington, D.C., Government Printing Office, 1941.
  1. Price Behavior and Business Policy, by Saul Nelson and Walter G. Keim.
  3. Who Pays the Taxes? by Gerhard Colm and Helen Tarasov.
  5. Industrial Wage Rates, Labor Costs and Price Policies, by Douglass V. Brown and others.
  8. Toward More Housing, by Peter A. Stone.
  9. Taxation of Corporate Enterprise, by C. J. Hynning.
  12. Profits, Productive Activities and New Investment, by Martin Taitel.
  16. Antitrust in Action, by Walton Hamilton and Irene Till.
  20. Taxation, Recovery and Defense, by H. Dewey Anderson.
  21. Competition and Monopoly in American Industry, by Claire Wilcox.
  22. Technology in Our Economy, by H. Dewey Anderson.
  31. Patents and Free Enterprise, by Walton Hamilton.
  32. Economic Standards of Government Price Control, by Ben W. Lewis and others.
  37. Saving, Investment, and National Income, by Oscar L. Altman.
  38. A Study of the Construction and Enforcement of the Federal Antitrust Law, by Milton Handler.

—— Final Report and Recommendations, verbatim record of statements of Senator O'Mahoney and others.

—— Final Report of the Executive Secretary, by H. Dewey Anderson and others.

—— Hearings, Part 9 "A Banking System for Capital and Capital Credit."

United States, Work Projects Administration. Industrial Change and Em-

BIBLIOGRAPHY

ployment Opportunity—a Selected Bibliography. Philadelphia, Pa., National Research Project, 1939.
United States, Works Progress Administration. Urban Workers on Relief. Division of Social Research, 1936. Research Monograph IV.
—— Progress Reports. Washington, D.C., 1936–1941.
Villard, Henry H. Deficit Spending and the National Income. New York, Farrar and Rinehart, 1941.
Webb, Sidney, and Beatrice Webb. English Poor Law History. London, Longmans, Green and Company, 1927.
Wicksell, Knut. Lectures on Political Economy. New York, Macmillan, 1934.
Williams, Edward A. Federal Aid for Relief. New York, Columbia University Press, 1939.
Williams, J. K. Grants in Aid under the Public Works Administration. New York, Columbia University Press, 1939.
Wolman, Leo. Planning and Control of Public Works. New York, National Bureau of Economic Research, 1930.
Wright, David McC. The Creation of Purchasing Power. Cambridge, Mass., Harvard University Press, 1942.

PAMPHLETS AND ARTICLES IN PERIODICALS

"American Institute of Public Opinion Surveys, 1938–1939," *Public Opinion Quarterly*, III, No. 4 (October, 1939), 581–607.
Applegate, La Rue. "Long Postponed Additions to Power Plant Capacity Reviving Equipment Sales," *Annalist*, L (July 2, 1937), 6–7.
Bielschowsky, George. "Business Fluctuations and Public Works," *Quarterly Journal of Economics*, XLIV (February, 1930), 286–319.
Bresciani-Turroni, C. "The Multiplier in Practice; Some Results of Recent German Experience," *Review of Economic Statistics*, XX (May, 1938), 76–88.
Clark, J. M. "Aggregate Spending by Public Works," *American Economic Review*, XXV (March, 1935), 14–20.
—— "An Appraisal of the Workability of Compensatory Devices," *American Economic Review*, XXIX (Supplement, March, 1939), 194–208.
Commercial and Financial Chronicle, "Forecasting a Permanent Dole," CXLI (September 21, 1935), 1829–1831.
—— "Looking Backward and Forward at Work Relief," CXLI (August 24, 1935), 1149–1151.
Copeland, Morris A. "Public Investment in the United States," *American Economic Review*, XXIX (Supplement, March, 1939), 33–41.
Crum, W. L. "Review of the Year 1936," *Review of Economic Statistics*, XIX (February, 1937), 27–36.
Davison, R. C. "Unemployment Relief in Germany," *Economic Journal*, XV (March, 1930), 140–146.
Dickinson, F. G. "Public Construction and Cyclical Unemployment,"

American Academy of Political and Social Science, *Annals*, Supplement, September, 1928.
Dirks, F. C. "Retail Sales and Labor Income," *Review of Economic Statistics*, XX (August, 1938), 128–134.
Economist (London) "Full Employment: the Aim," CXLIII (October 3, 1942), 407–408.
——— "Full Employment: the Means," CXLIII (October 10, 1942), 438–440.
——— "Full Employment: the Cost," CXLIII (October 17, 1942), 472–473.
——— "Humbug of Finance, The," CXL (May 3, 1941), 579–580.
Ellis, Howard S. "Monetary Policy and Investment," *American Economic Review*, XXX (Supplement, March, 1940), 27–38.
Ezekiel, Mordecai. "The Cobweb Theorem," *Quarterly Journal of Economics*, LII (February, 1938), 255–280.
Fleming, J. M. "Secular Unemployment," *Quarterly Journal of Economics*, LIV (November, 1939), 103–130.
Fortune, Poll, XIX, No. 3 (March, 1939), 132–135.
Gayer, Arthur D. "Fiscal Policies," *American Economic Review*, XXVIII (Supplement, March, 1938), 90–112.
Gilbert, Donald W. "Taxation and Economic Stability," *Quarterly Journal of Economics*, LVI (May, 1942), 406–429.
Gilboy, E. W. "The Propensity to Consume," *Quarterly Journal of Economics*, LIII (November, 1938), 120–140.
Gordon, R. A. "Fiscal Policy as a Factor in Stability," American Academy of Political and Social Science, *Annals*, CCVI (November, 1939), 106–113.
Graham, Frank. "Partial Reserve Money and the One Hundred Percent Proposal," American Economic Review, XXVI (September, 1936), 428–440.
Grebler, Leo. "Housing Policy and the Building Cycle," *Review of Economic Statistics*, XXIV (May, 1942), 66–74.
Hansen, Alvin H. "Progress and Declining Population," *American Economic Review*, XXIX (March, 1939), 1–15.
Hansen, Alvin H., and Guy Greer. "Toward Full Use of Our Resources," *Fortune*, XXVI, No. 5 (November, 1942), 130–133, 158–178.
Hansen, Alvin H., and Harvey S. Perloff. "Regional Resource Development," National Planning Association, Pamphlet No. 16, October, 1942.
Hoyt, Kendall K. "Business Sectors Likely to Be Benefited by Works Relief Appropriation," *Annalist*, XLV (April 19, 1935), 584–585.
——— "Probable Effect on Business of Beginning of Five Billion Relief Program," XLVI (July 19, 1935), 74.
Humphrey, Don D. "The Nature and Meaning of Rigid Prices, 1890–1933," *Journal of Political Economy*, XLV (October, 1937), 651–661.
Kahn, R. F. "Public Works and Inflation," *Journal American Statistical Association*, XXVIII (Supplement, March, 1933), 168–173.

—— "The Relation of Home Investment to Unemployment," *Economic Journal*, XLI (June, 1931), 173–198.
Key, V. O. "The Lack of a Budget Theory," *American Political Science Review*, LV (December, 1940), 1137–1147.
Keynes, J. M. "Fluctuations in Net Investment in the United States," *Economic Journal*, XLVI (September, 1936), 540–547.
—— "Relative Movements of Real Wages and Output," *Economic Journal*, XLIX (March, 1939), 34–51.
—— review of Tinbergen's *Statistical Testing of Business-Cycle Theories, I*, in *Economic Journal*, XLIX (September, 1939), 558–568.
Kindleberger, Charles P. "Planning for Foreign Investment," *American Economic Review*, XXXIII (Supplement, March, 1943), 347–354.
Kreps, T. J. "Consumption a Vast Under-developed Economic Frontier," *American Economic Review*, XXX (Supplement, February, 1941), 177–199.
Kuznets, Simon. "National Income and Taxable Capacity," *American Economic Review*, XXXII (Supplement, March, 1942), 37–75.
Lange, Oscar. "The Rate of Interest and the Optimum Propensity to Consume," *Economica*, V (February, 1938), 12–32.
McConnell, B. M. "The Press Looks at Pump Priming," *Current History*, XLVIII (June, 1938), 30–32.
Machlup, Fritz. "Period Analysis and Multiplier Theory," *Quarterly Journal of Economics*, LIV (November, 1939), 1–27.
Mason, Edward S. "Price Inflexibility," *Review of Economic Statistics*, XX (May, 1938), 53–64.
Means, Gardiner C. "Price Inflexibility and the Requirements of a Stabilizing Monetary Policy," *Journal of the American Statistical Association*, XXX (June, 1935), 401–413.
Mills, F. C. "Relation of Size of Plants to Prices—Discussion," *American Economic Review*, XXVI (Supplement, March, 1936), 62–64.
Mitnitzky, M. "The Effects of a Public Works Policy on Business Activity and Employment," *International Labor Review*, XXX (October, 1934), 435–456.
Morgenthau, Henry. "Federal Spending and the Federal Budget," *Proceedings of Academy of Political Science*, XVII, No. 4 (January, 1938), 534–542.
Musgrave, R. A. "Budgetary Balance and Capital Budget," *American Economic Review*, XXIX (June, 1939), 260–271.
Musgrave, R. A., and B. M. Higgins. "Theoretical Basis of Public Spending," in *Public Policy*, Cambridge, Mass., Harvard University Press. Vol. II. 1941.
Myrdal, Gunnar. "Fiscal Policy in the Business Cycle," *American Economic Review*, XXIX (Supplement, March, 1939), 183–193.
—— "The Swedish Budget," *Fortune*, XVIII, No. 3 (September, 1938), 65–66, 130–145.

National Industrial Conference Board. *Economic Record*, New York, 1939–1940, *passim*.
National Planning Association. "International Development Loans," Washington, D.C., 1942. Pamphlet No. 15.
Opie, Redvers. Address delivered before the American Marketing Association, reported in the New York *Times*, February 26, 1943.
Ratchford, B. U. "The Burden of a Domestic Debt," *American Economic Review*, XXXII (September, 1942), 451–467.
Robbins, Lionel. "The Long-Term Budget Problem," *Lloyds Bank Monthly Review*, New Series IX, No. 98 (April, 1938), 158–167.
Samuelson, Paul A. "Interactions between the Multiplier Analysis and the Principle of Acceleration," *Review of Economic Statistics*, XX (May, 1939), 75–78.
——— "A Synthesis of the Principle of Acceleration and the Multiplier," *Journal of Political Economy*, XLV (December, 1939), 786–797.
——— "The Theory of Pump-Priming Reexamined," *American Economic Review*, XXX (September, 1940), 492–506.
Seltzer, Lawrence. "Direct versus Fiscal and Institutional Factors," *American Economic Review*, XXX (February, 1941), 99–107.
Simons, Henry C. "Hansen on Fiscal Policy," *Journal of Political Economy*, L (April, 1942), 161–196.
——— A Positive Program for Laissez-Faire. Chicago, University of Chicago Press, 1934.
Slichter, Sumner H. "The Conditions of Expansion," *American Economic Review*, XXXII (Supplement, March, 1942), 1–21.
——— "The Downturn of 1937," *Review of Economic Statistics*, XX (August, 1938), 97–110.
——— "The Economics of Public Works," *American Economic Review*, XXIV (Supplement, March, 1934), 174–185.
——— "The Period 1919–1936 in the United States: Its Significance for Business Cycle Theory," *Review of Economic Statistics*, XIX (February, 1937), 1–19.
——— "Postwar Boom or Collapse," *Harvard Business Review*, XXI (autumn, 1942), 5–42.
Smith, Dan T. "An Analysis of Changes in Federal Finances, July, 1930–June, 1938," *Review of Economic Statistics*, XX (November, 1938), 149–160.
Sweezy, A. R. "Population Growth and Investment Opportunity," *Quarterly Journal of Economics*, LV (November, 1940), 64–79.
Tucker, Rufus S. "The Essential Historical Facts about 'Sensitive' and 'Administered' Prices," *Annalist*, LI (February 4, 1938), 195–196.
Turner, T. J. "The Significance of the Frontier in American History," Forty-First Annual Meeting of the State Historical Society of Wisconsin, December 14, 1893.
United States, Department of Agriculture. *The Agricultural Situation*, January 1, 1938. Washington, D.C., Government Printing Office, 1938.

BIBLIOGRAPHY

United States, Department of Commerce. *Survey of Current Business* (monthly). Washington, D.C., Government Printing Office, 1937–1943, *passim*.

United States, Federal Reserve Board. *Federal Reserve Bulletin* (monthly). 1930–1942 *passim*.

United States, President's Message Transmitting the Budget, Fiscal Years 1930 through 1941. Washington, D.C., Government Printing Office.

United States Senate, Special Committee to Investigate Unemployment and Relief (Senator Burns, chairman). [Report.] Senate Report No. 1625, 75th Congr., 3d Sess., April 20, 1938.

United States, Social Security Board. *Social Security Bulletin* (monthly). 1937–1940 *passim*.

"United States in a New World, The," *Fortune* (Supplement for December, Vol. XXVI, No. 6. 1942).

Viner, Jacob. Balanced Deflation, Inflation, or More Depression. Minneapolis, University of Minnesota Press, 1933. Day and Hour Series, No. 3.

Wallace, Donald H. Industrial Markets and Public Policy. Public Policy. Cambridge, Mass., Harvard University Press, 1940. Vol. I.

Williams, John H. "Federal Budget: Economic Consequences of Deficit Financing," *American Economic Review*, XXX, No. 5 (February, 1941), 52–66.

——— "The Implications of Fiscal Policy for Monetary Policy and the Banking System," *American Economic Review*, XXXII (Supplement, March, 1942), 234–249.

Wood, Ralph C. "Tucker's 'Reasons' of Price Rigidity," *American Economic Review*, XXVIII (December, 1938), 663–673.

Wright, David McC. "The Economic Limit and Economic Burden of an Internally Held National Debt," *Quarterly Journal of Economics*, LV (November, 1940), 116–129.

INDEX

Acceleration principle, 14, 16, 97, 115
Adams, H. C., quoted, 6
Agricultural adjustment, *see* Farmers
Agricultural Adjustment Act, 89
Angell, J. W., quoted, 50, 77
Arnold, Thurman, 129, 151 f.
"Asset, public," term, 41

Baikie, J., quoted, 9n
Banking system, central banking policy, 2, 3, 86; capital credit banks, 56; Hundred Percent Reserve Plan, 71, 79, 84; possible need for greater control over, 73; Federal Reserve banks, 78, 116; program that would revolutionize, 79; 1933 rehabilitation, 89; postwar restrictive policy, 148
Berle, A. A., Jr., 56
Bibliography, 161-69
Birth rate, conscious reduction of, 62, 63
Bonds, goverment, 68
Bonus, veterans', 101, 103, 104 f.; Christmas, 106
Bowley, A. L., 9, 11
Bowman, Isaiah, 63
Budget, cyclical balance, 23, 27, 39; capital-current budget, 40-44, 81 ff.; challenges to classical budgetary tradition, 67, 72, 73, 79, 118; groups attacking change, 83, 99, 120; orthodoxy during Hoover administration, 86, 87; forces compelling expansionist policy, 88; during Roosevelt administration, 95, 99-101, 117 f., 125; Morganthau's ideas and plans, 117; postwar, 142
Building construction, *see* Construction
Building material, prices, 129
Burns, A. E., and D. S. Watson, quoted, 127n
Business and industry, saturation factors, 45, 46; response to labor's new power, 50; impact of increased tax burdens, 50 ff.; corporate tax changes before and following first World War, 51; psychological reaction and policy during the thirties, 53; attitude toward Roosevelt administration: resistance to change, 53 f.; technological innovation, 55 f., 146, 155; opposition to budget deficits, 83, 99, 120; NRA effect upon, 90; production chart, 93; recovery of 1936, 101-7; failure to appraise bonus spending correctly, 105; inventory accumulation, 105, 109 ff.; large dividends and bonus gifts, 106n; review of major economic series, 1929-37, 108 ff.; partial conversion to expansionist public spending, 120; weight of tax program upon investment, 127 (*see also* Taxation); monopoly control, 129, 151 ff.; restrictive price and trade practices, 130, 152; problem of postwar reconversion, 144, 147; accumulated backlog of demand: contributing factors: foreign shortages, 145; resulting market, 148; problem of resolving business-labor policies, 154; postwar private enterprise or government investment? 156 ff.; *see also* Consumption; Economic progress; Investment; Private enterprise
Business cycle, *see* Depression
Buying power, national: net contribution of government to, charts, 92 f. See Krost-Currie series

Capital, marginal efficiency of, and demand for, 15, 31, 33, 47; "shortage of capital" school, 29; period of rise in capital formation, 35; discouraged by corporate tax structure, 51; dominating influence of investment in a single industry, 55; distribution of gross national product, 141 ff.; postwar: national income goal, 144; provision of international, 158, 159
Capital and current expenditures, distinction between, 38, 41
Capital credit banks, 56
Capital-current budget, 40-44, 81 ff.
Capital goods industries, effect of government orders upon, 22
Capitalism, failure to provide stability or security: future of, 1
Cassel, Gustav, 34
Catchings, W., W. T. Foster and, quoted, 31
Central banking, *see* Banking
Change, resistance of business to, 53, 54, 86

INDEX

Civil Work Administration, 95, 96, 103, 104, 121, 124; more than a relief program, 90; objective: statistics of outlays, 91; when terminated, 94, 99

Clark, J. M., 13, 17, 22n, 42, 153

Compensatory public spending, meaning and goal, 36-39, 118; budget system, 42, 81, 118 (*see also* Budget); retirement from: susceptibility to cyclical manipulation, 43; potential scope of, as revealed by spending experience of the thirties, 115, 124 ff.; as sole answer to problem of idle resources, 127, 128

"Competition, imperfect," 152

Competition as monopoly control, 155

Construction, relation of population growth to residential, 57, 60; importance to industry, of PWA program, 97; table of expenditures: decline in state and local, 98; private housing activity, 129; public expenditures, 1921-41, 134; chart, 135; relative importance of private to public: ratio of expenditures, with chart, 136-38; need of co-ordinating operations of different governmental layers, 136; self-liquidating residential construction, 139; postwar residential building, 148 ff.

Consume, propensity to, 15, 31 ff.

Consumer credit financing, 105, 110, 114

Consumption, relationship between increments of investment and, 3, 15; dependence of pump-priming success upon induced, 22 ff.; underconsumption or oversaving theory, 29 ff.; effects of deficiency in consumer purchasing power, 30, 118; consumer subsidies, 37; distinction between potential and effective demand, 58; in the three levels of income groups, 59; relation to standard of living, 62; tax proposals re increasing, 71; effects upon: relief payments, 96; PWA wages, 98; veterans' bonus, 101, 103, 104 f.; consumer purchasing upon 1936 recovery: factors responsible for it, 106, 114

Corporate dividends, largest ever paid, 106n

Corporation taxes, 51, 70, 146

Credit, easing of situation, 13, 116; capital credit banks, 56; consumer credit financing, 105, 110, 114

Current expenditures, *see* Capital and current

Debt, public: government outlays to be financed by additions to, 2; size limits, 5, 70, 71, 74, 76 ff.; growth of, held desirable, 39, 67; budget changes, 40, 42, 67; capital-current budget, 40-44, 81 ff.; Hansen's analysis of role of, and limits to, 67-85; evaluation of the burden incidental to internally held debt, 67 ff.; early opposition to, 67, 73; an instrument of public policy, 67, 81; classification: character of outlay, 68; effects of tax structure, 68, 70 ff., 75, 83; effect upon level of employment and standard of living, 69; interest, 71, 75 f., 79, 82, 84, 143; relativity of, 73-80; expansion from 1790: dismay over, during the thirties, 74; contrast in attitudes toward depression and war debt, 75; less painful than tax financing: why opposed, 76; mechanical obstacles to protracted accumulation, 77 ff.; competition with private enterprise, 80-85; socializing influence, 81; estimated total at war's end: annual interest bill, 143n; fiscal solvency in face of postwar level? 157; *see also* Loans

Defense expenditures, *see* War

Deferred demand, and foreign shortages, 145; resulting postwar market, 148

Deficit financing, *see* Budget; Debt

Demobilization, 142, 143, 148, 150

Democracies, cannot return to prewar status: problem of postwar reconstruction, 1; population demands, 7

Denmark, budgetary procedure, 41, 82n

Depression, chronic, *see* Secular-stagnation;
—— of 1921-22, 10
—— of the thirties, pessimism, 1, 53, 54; causes, 30, 53 ff., 118; influence of price disparities in shaping business cycle, 47, 49; public debt arising out of, 74 (*see also* Debt); conquest by Hoover's policies; European recovery, 87; *see also* Recession; Recovery
—— threat of postwar, 141

Development and Road Funds Act of Great Britain, 9

Dividends, corporate: largest ever made, 106n

Dwellings, *see* Construction

Eccles, Marriner S., 118

Economic maturity, 2, 35, 55

Economic philosophy of Roosevelt administration, 116 f., 125

Economic policy, postwar, 141-59; *see* entries *under* Postwar

Economic progress, theories, 34; period of

INDEX

intensive growth, 35; significance of altered rate of population growth, 35, 56-63; analysis of factors responsible for: role of technological progress, 45-56; outlook for technological innovation, 55, 146; limits of economic penetration into undeveloped areas, 63-66; postwar business, 65, 145 ff.

Economic series, major: ten-year review, 108 ff.

Economist, The, excerpt, 127

Egypt, earliest public works relief, 8n

Emergency Banking Act, 89

Employment, public works as employment-creating schemes, 8; British works to stabilize, 9; secondary, 13; relation principle in theory of, 14; effect of deficit financing upon level of, 69; under WPA program, 96, 120, 121, 124; spending geared to variations in private, 96, 121; scale of outlays required for full, 127 f.; *see also* Unemployment

Employment multiplier, 14n

Expenditures, distinction between capital and current, 38, 41; *see also* Public spending

Farmers, relief demanded, 88; cash income, chart, 93; agricultural adjustment and farm credit aids, 94

Federal Emergency Relief Administration, 90, 94, 95, 96, 97, 125

Federal Reserve banks, 78, 116

Financial institutions, legal limitations upon funds: proposed remedy, 56; holdings of government issues: controls over, 73; *see also* Banking

Fiscal policy, emergence, 2 f., 6-28; of Hoover and Roosevelt administrations, 86 ff.; 1937-38 monetary policy, 116 ff.; most successful measures, 121; as adjunct to spending measures, 125; role in postwar economic policy, 141 ff.

Fluctuations, control of short-run price and economic, 78

Foreign loans, 1921-29, 65; postwar, 158

Foreign postwar rehabilitation, 146

Fortune, excerpt, 155n

Foster, W. T., and W. Catchings, quoted, 31

France, franc crisis, 102

Freedom, choice between security and, 1

Frontier, disappearance of, 64

Gayer, A. D., quoted, 7

General Theory of Employment, Interest and Money (Keynes), 3, 14, 30, 31

Gilbert, D. W., on tax ratio, 126

Gold sterilization, 116

Government, investment, etc., *see under* Public

"Government investment," term, 38

Great Britain, public works, 9, 11; finance, 39n, 69, 127; residential building, 130; postwar reconversion of industry, 144n, 147

Gross national product, distribution, 141 ff.

Growth, cessation of, 34; intensive, 35; *see also* Economic progress

Haberler, G. von, 30

Hamilton, Walton, and Irene Till, quoted, 152

Hansen, Alvin H., 17n, 22, 25n, 39n, 143, 144n; secular-stagnation doctrine, 1 f., 29, 34-36; critique of his doctrine, 45-66; analysis of factors of economic progress, 45 ff.; views on significance of population growth, 56 ff.; analysis of limits and role of economic penetration, 63 ff.; of role of public debt, 67-85; relation of tax structure to it, 68, 70 ff.; faith in compensatory public spending (*q.v.*), as answer to problem of idle resources, 127, 128

—— and Harvey S. Perloff, 155n

Harris, S. S., 78; quoted, 5

Harrod, R. F., 16

Hicks, Mrs. U. K., 68

Home Owners Loan Corporation, 129

Hoover, Herbert, 138; quoted: policies, 87

Hoover administration, 86, 88, 89; banking policy, 3

Housing, market conditions: postwar boom, 149; *see also* Construction

Hundred Percent Reserve Plan, 71, 79, 84

Ideology of spending, 130-32

Immigration, economic consequences of population increase from, 60-62

Income, created by public spending, loss through leakages, 14; successive stages produced by public outlays, 16 ff.; and wealth, inequality of distribution, 30, 71; federal payments and cash farm income, chart, 93; total portion attributable to governmental goods and services: distribution of gross national product, 141 ff.; prospects for postwar realization of enlarged, 143, 144 ff.; cost-price relationships in income determination, 154

Income-decreasing taxes, 113 f.

Income taxes, 51, 70, 71, 113

INDEX

Industry, see Business and industry
Inflation, 43, 116; controls, 72, 78; during 1936–37, 78; in prospect in 1933, 89, 90; postwar danger of, 146, 147, 148, 149, 157
Insurance, unemployment, 150, 155
Interest on public debt, 82; elimination of, 71, 79, 84; relation of taxes to, 75 f.; postwar, 143
International economic policy, postwar, 157-59
International tension, effect upon business, 54, 102
International trade and economic relations, 131 f.
Inventions, see Technological
Inventories, accumulation, 105, 109 ff.
Investment, relationship between increments of, and consumption, 3, 15; stimulation of private, as pump-priming goal, 13; net increment of, 15, 16 ff.; dependence of pump-priming success upon induced, 22 ff.; dependence of employment upon increase in, 32; relationship between public and private activity, 36, 43; meaning of "government investment," 38; productive and nonproductive, 41; significance for, altered rate of population growth, 56-63; pessimism over prospects for outlets: causes and remedy, 56; effects of limits of economic penetration into undeveloped areas, 63-66; weight of tax program, 127; see also Private enterprise
Investment multiplier, 14n

Justice Department, Anti-Trust Division, 129, 151

Kahn, R. F., "relation" principle, 14
Keynes, J. M., place of fiscal operations in analysis by, 3; psychological propensities, 3, 15, 31; the Kahn "relation" adopted, 14; use of multiplier, 15 ff.; estimates re federal expenditure changes, 21; allegiance to underconsumption theory, 30, 32; analytical system examined: on unemployment, 31-34
King, W. I., 63
Krost-Currie series, 91, 103, 112, 113
Kuznets, Simon, 110n; quoted: tax statistics, 52

Labor, institutional controls over wages: business response to new power of, 50, 53; immigrant labor, 60 ff.; capacity of the economy to absorb, 61; opposition to altering price practices, 130; problem of postwar readjustment, 144, 147; responsibilities of organized, 153 f.; see also Employment; Unemployed; Wages
Legal limitations upon funds of financial institutions, 56
Limits of Land Settlement, Bowman's report on, 63
Liquidity-preference, 15, 31
Loans, foreign, 1921–29, 65; postwar, 158
Loans, government: category of, 12; effects, 13; self-liquidating, 86, 103, 119, 138; results of large-scale lending, 129; see also Debt
London Economic Conference, 90, 131
Lundberg, Erik, 27

"Marginal multiplier time interval," 17
Maturity, economic, 2, 34, 35, 55
Military expenditures, see War
Military forces, demobilization, 142, 143, 148, 150
Mill, John Stuart, 35
Mills, F. C., quoted, 49n
Monetary policy, see Fiscal policy
Monopolies, antitrust activities, 129, 151 f.; Roosevelt's message on, 151n; recommended controls, 152 f., 155n
Morgenthau, Henry, quoted, 117
Multiplier concept, 3, 14-22; logical theory of, 16, 20; properties, 16 ff.
Myrdal, Gunnar, 41, 82n

Nathan, Robert R., 102n
National Labor Relations Act, 53
National Recovery Act, first effects, 89; codes: boom and collapse, 90
National Resources Planning Board, WPA expenditures table, 98; quoted, 128n, 133, 136, 139n; federal construction, charts, 135, 137; regional resource development plans, 155
Net increment of investment, 15, 16 ff.
New Deal, see Roosevelt administration
Nugent, Rolf, quoted, 110n

Office of Price Administration, price ceilings, 148
100 percent reserve banking notes, 71, 79, 84
Opie, Redvers, 144n
Oversaving or underconsumption theory, 29 ff.

Perloff, Harvey S., and A. H. Hansen, 155n

INDEX

Pessimism, during depression, 1, 53, 54; Hansen's, over prospects of investment outlets, 56

Philosophy, economic: of Roosevelt administration, 116, 125

Pigou, A. C., 37

Planning, public works, *see* Public works

"Policy" fiscal: as applied to New Deal spending, 3n; *see also* Fiscal policy

Political considerations, influence and effect, 28, 53, 99, 130

Political sabotage, attacks against spending related to, 75

Population growth, significance of altered rate, 35, 56-63; through immigration, 60 ff.

Postwar world, apprehension over future of, 1, 141; technological change, 55, 146; U.S. foreign investment, 65; outlook for extension of public debt, 75; role of fiscal policy in economic policy, 141 ff.; short-run problem, 141-44; prospects for utilization of resources and realization of enlarged national income, 144-47; economic environment, 145; immediate problems and government policy in transition period, 147-50; conditions in building field, 149; post-transitional period, 151-54; role of public spending, 154-57; international economic policy, 157-59

President's Conference on Unemployment, 1921, 10

Press, campaigns of opposition to public spending, debt, 83, 99, 120n

Pressure groups, 7

Prices, relation to economic progress, 46 ff.; to business cycle, 47, 49; functioning of system since first World War, 48; administered, 49; 1936–37 index: effects, 108 f., 110, 114; no satisfactory reconstruction program for system as a whole, 129, 152; restrictive practices, 130, 151n, 152; postwar control, 148

Private enterprise, decline, 2; relationship between public and private investment activity, 2, 36, 39, 43, 80-85, 136-38; economic leadership relinquished, 86; postwar responsibilities, 156, 159; alternative to failure, 157; building construction, *see* Construction; Investment

Propensity to consume, 15, 31 ff.

Protective tariff and foreign debt, 65

Psychological causes of depression, 53

Psychological predispositions in the Keynesian analysis, 3, 15

Psychology, factors in the business picture, 1, 12, 122

"Public asset," term, 41

Public spending, relationship between private enterprise and, 2, 36, 39, 43, 80-85, 136-38; emergence as chief instrument of New Deal recovery policy, 3; short of magnitude required for recovery, 4, 127 f.; changing concepts of: economic justification, 6; changes effecting expenditure patterns, 6 f.; secondary effects, 14 ff.; Keynes's estimates of consequences of changes in, 21; timing, 24, 26 f., 37, 115; reversals of policy in U.S., 27; compensatory, 36-39, 42, 43, 81, 115, 118, 124 ff.; contrast in public attitude toward depression and war expenditures, 75; evaluation of influence of Roosevelt administration's policy and program, 86-140 *passim* (*see entries under* Roosevelt administration); net contribution to national buying power, charts, 92 f.; measurement of 1936–37 expenditures vs. tax receipts, with table, 112 ff.; spending and lending program after 1937 recession, 116 ff.; polls showing attitude of newspapers and public, 121n; role in postwar world, 154-57

Public utilities, self-liquidating projects, 139; competition in field of, 155

Public works, defined, 7n; effects of growing demand for, 7; planning, 8-12, 134; timing, 8, 10, 133; in ancient Egypt, 8n; in Great Britain, 9, 11; difficulties in early schemes, 9; heavy large-scale projects not postponable, 10 f.; in 1921–22 depression, 10; pump-priming, 12-14, 22-28, 94, 104; Roosevelt administration's program, 90-140 *passim;* expenditure statistics, 91 (charts, 135, 137); emergency public works appraised: objects of expenditure, 133-36; self-liquidating projects, 138 f.; feasibility of large postwar program, 148; should not have responsibility for short-term unemployment: regional resource development, 155; *see also under* Roosevelt administration; *and the projects, e.g.,* PWA, WPA, *etc.*

Public Works Administration, 50, 90, 94, 96, 104, 124, 133; why rejected in favor of WPA, 99; program hampered by delays, 134

Pump-priming, 12-14, 22-28, 104; two-phase program, 12; effects of spending, and loans, 12, 13; flexibility: stages: goal, 13; financing the program, 23, 27; basis of

INDEX

Pump-priming (*continued*)
decisions as to timing and type, 24, 26; conditions necessary for success, 94

Railroads, 155n; capital investment in, 55; PWA loans to, 94n
Ratchford, B. V., quoted, 76
Recession of 1937, causal factors analyzed, 27, 78, 107-15, 118; importance of price developments, 47, 49; review of major economic series preceding, 108 ff.; 1936-37 expenditures and tax receipts, with table, 112 ff.; reversal of monetary policy, 115; spending and lending program, the main burden of attack on, 116 ff.; *see also* Depression of the thirties
Reciprocal Trade Agreements Policy, 131
Reconstruction Finance Corporation, loans, 86, 103, 119, 138
Recovery of 1936, veterans' bonus and other causative factors, 101-7; developments in field of consumer credit, 105
Recovery program, superseded by defense and war expenditures, 4, 122 f., 125; domestic type, 131
Regional Resource Development (Hansen and Perloff), 155
"Relation," term, 14, 16
"Relation of Home Investment to Unemployment, The" (Kahn), 14
Relation principle, 14 ff.
Relief, government spending primarily for, 3n; groups demanding, 87; projects of Roosevelt administration, 90-140 *passim*; problem turned over to states, 95; relief and recovery program after 1937 recession, 116 ff.; dominant influence on pattern of work projects, 133; *see also under* Roosevelt administration; *and the projects, e.g.*, CWA, FERA, *etc.*
Republican administrations, relations with business, 54; fiscal orthodoxy, 87, 88
Roosevelt, Franklin D., quoted, 89n, 100 f., 118, 151n; reason for 1932 election victory, 88; budgetary doctrine, 100, 118, 125; spending and lending program advocated, 116, 117
Roosevelt administration, New Deal economic policy and results, 2, 3 f.; recovery policy shadowed by defense and war programs, 4, 122 f., 125; 1937 recession, 27, 47, 49, 78, 107-15, 116 ff.; appraisal of its tax measures, 51, 126; attitude of business toward: chief subjects of its criticism, 53 f., 83, 99, 120; valuation of the influence of policy upon business activity, 86-123; from inauguration to WPA, 88-95; deficits and budgets, 95, 99-101, 118, 125; creation and meaning of WPA (*q.v.*), 95-99; 1936 subsidized recovery, 101-7; monetary and fiscal policy: spending program; results, 115-22; inner conflict re fiscal and budgetary philosophy, 116, 125; most successful monetary and fiscal measures, 121; lessons of New Deal spending, 124-40; results of compensatory fiscal policy, 124; appraisal of its spending policy, 126-32; of emergency public works, 133-40; self-liquidating projects, 138 f.

Samuelson, Paul A., 16n, 25
Saturation, industrial: technological, 45 ff.
Saving, marginal propensity to save: multiplier the reciprocal of, 15; oversaving or underconsumption theory, 29 ff.; when not injurious, 31
Savings, drained by income tax, 71; tax ratio relative to, 126
Scandinavian countries, budget experience, 40, 41, 82n
Schumpeter, J. A., 34, 70
"Secondary employment," 13, 15
Secular-stagnation thesis, of Alvin Hansen, 1 f., 29 ff., 34-36; defined, 36; place of compensatory public spending in theory of, 36-39; critique of, 45-66; economic progress and technological saturation, 45-56; population growth and new investment, '56-63; investment opportunities and the limits of economic penetration, 63-66; views on debt integrally related to, 67
Security exchange regulations, 53
Self-liquidating loans, 86, 103, 119, 138
—— public projects, 138 f.
Sherman Act, 151, 152
Simons, H. C., 80, 81
Slichter, S. H., 25; quoted, 50; estimates of postwar demands, 145 f.
Smith, Adam, 6, 29n
Socialization of our economy? 80, 81
Social objectives of New Deal taxes, 51
Social responsibilities and pressure, 28
Social Security Act, 53, 150
Social security for military forces, 150
Social Security taxes, 113, 114, 115, 126
Social unrest as challenge to fiscal policy, 88
Spanish Civil War, 102
Spiethoff, A. A. C., 34
Stagnation thesis, defined, 36; *see also* Secular stagnation

INDEX

Standard of living, effect upon consumption, 62; rise in U.S., 63; effect of deficit financing upon, 69; WPA relief beneficiaries, 96

States, federal grants to, 10; relief problem turned over to, 95; construction appropriations of localities and, 98, 104, 136

Stuart and Bowley, public works planning, 11

Subsidized residential building, 149

Survey of Current Business, 142

Sweden, budget, 41, 82n; self-liquidating investment, 139

Tariff, protective: and foreign debt, 65

Taxation, relation between New Deal tax and spending policies, 4, 126 f.; effects of regressive, 23, 69, 114; impact of increase, upon business, 50 ff., 84; rates of increase, 1909–39, 51 f.; social objectives of New Deal measures, 51; corporation taxes, 51, 70, 146; reasons for world-wide increases, 52; relation to public debt, 68, 70, 75, 78, 83; burden of nonprogressive tax, 68; problem of taxable capacity: significant variables involved, 70 ff., 78, 83, 84; transformation of conventional approach to, 71; why borrowing less painful, 76; transfer charges: nontransfer expenditures, 83 f.; 1936–37 tax receipts and federal expenditures, with table, 112 ff.; to what extent income decreasing? 113; on income earned at source, 148; postwar overhauling of revenue system needed, 154

Technological innovation, number and variety, 47; promising outlook, 55 f., 146; resulting market, 148; public utilities, 155

Technological progress: role of, and dependence of economic activity upon, 45-56

Temporary National Economic Committee, 130, 152

Tennessee Valley Authority, 133, 155

Till, Irene, and Walton Hamilton, quoted, 152

Time intervals, average and marginal, distinguished, 17n

Timing, public works outlays, 8, 10, 133; pump-priming program, 13, 24, 26; public spending program, 24, 26, 37, 115; of retrenchment, 26 f.; compensatory program, 44

Tinbergen, J., 27

Trade, postwar international, 158, 159; see also Business and industry

Treasury Department, sterilization program, 116; *Bulletin*, table of defense expenditures, 122

Trusts, antitrust prosecutions, 129, 151 f.

Tugan-Baranowski, M., 34

Turner, T. J., 64n

Underconsumption or oversaving theory, 29 ff.

Unemployment Insurance Act, 50

Unemployment, amount during depression of the thirties, 4, 102n, 108, 124; Egypt's earliest relief, 9n; during 1921–22 depression, 10; Keynes's analysis of, 31-34; demands for relief, 87, 88; lack of ability for public works activity: number who could have been absorbed, 138; demobilized military personnel, 143, 148, 150; postwar, 147, 148, 150; insurance and other protection, 150, 155; see also Employment; Relief

Unemployment Conference, 1921, 10

Veterans' bonus, 101, 103, 104 f.

Wages, increase in institutional controls over: effects, 50; gains during unemployment: effect of immigrant labor, 62; 1936–37 developments: effects, 108, 110; building trades, 129; alteration of price practices, 130; problem of wage-rate determination, 153 f.

Wages and Hours Act, 50, 53

War and defense expenditures, 4, 7, 122 f., 142, table, 122; postwar, 143; see also World War

Watson, D. S., A. E. Burns and, quoted, 127n

Wealth and income, inequality of distribution, 30, 71

Wicksell, Knut, 34

Williams, John H., quoted, 3n

Works Progress Administration, 38, 50, 103, 125, 134; study of technological change, 48; creation of, as FERA successor, 95; meaning of, as major basis of relief program, 95-99; effect upon consumer demand: upon construction industry, 97; reduction in outlays, 111, 121; statistics on progress, 112; rise in adjusted expenditures, 119 f.; only fraction of unemployed on payroll, 124

Works projects, see Public works

World War II, economic repercussions, 121-23; conditions culminating in, 131; see also War